The Mayfield Quick View Guide to the Internet
for Students of Psychology and the Research Process

VERSION 2.0

Angela Sadowski
Chaffey College

Jennifer Campbell Koella
University of Tennessee, Knoxville

Michael Keene
University of Tennessee, Knoxville

D1293406

Mayfield Publishing Company
Mountain View, California
London • Toronto

INTRODUCTION

The dream behind the Web is of a common information space in which we can communicate by sharing information. Its universality is essential: the fact that a hypertext link can point to anything, be it personal, local, or global, be it draft or highly published.

—Tim Berners-Lee, "Press FAQ." 7 December 1998
<http://www.w3.org/People/Berners-Lee/FAQ.html>

What Can the Internet Do for You?

*The **Internet** is a vast resource*—not only for information, entertainment, and interaction with other people in other places who share your interests, but also for learning. You can do everything from reading newspapers and magazines, to learning how to create your own Web page, to video-conferencing, to watching video clips from your favorite movies, to down-loading free software for your computer, to taking a virtual tour of Hawaii or Frank Lloyd Wright's house, Fallingwater. The Internet often has the most current news, the best views of the weather anywhere, the best maps, and up-to-the-minute discussions of current events. Additionally, it is convenient to have a variety of dictionaries, thesauri, and encyclopedias on hand while writing a paper.

Beyond all those uses, *the Internet frees you from the physical boundaries of your hometown, your campus, your city, your state, and your country.* Information from Japan or Germany or Australia can come to you just as fast and easily as information from across the hall. Because the Internet does not have opening or closing hours, its information is more accessible than the information in your library. (And, at many schools, more and more of the library's resources are available on the Internet.) Your school's library may be tiny, but with access to the Internet, you have more information at your fingertips than the biggest library anywhere. All you need to do is learn how to find it. To help you find information on the Internet quickly—and document it correctly—is the purpose of this book.

What Are the Internet and the World Wide Web?

The Internet is a global network of computers. It is composed of many parts, such as Web documents, e-mail, Telnet, file transfer, Usenet (newsgroups), and Gopher. Until the **World Wide Web** came along, the Internet was diffi-cult to use. *The Web is a huge number of sites of information within the Internet.*

1

Not only does the Web make accessing the Internet easier, but it also makes the Internet more fun because of the Web's **hypermedia** capabilities, such as audio, video, 3-D images, virtual reality, real-time communication, and animation. Sounds good, doesn't it? So let us help you get started!

QUICK VIEW
How Can I Use Graphic Access to the Internet?

Many students have access to computers that already have Netscape, Explorer, or some other graphic browser. If that's your situation, this page will get you off to a fast start. If you need to start from scratch, go to page 5 for more detailed directions.

Using Netscape and Other Graphic Browsers

To access the Web's multimedia capabilities, you need a graphic browser, such as Netscape or Microsoft's Internet Explorer. (*Note:* You also need TCP/IP software; see page 5.) Netscape is used in the following description; other browsers, such as Explorer, work in essentially the same way.

Click on the Netscape icon to launch the program. The first page you see will depend on your ISP (Internet service provider). Most providers have designated a Web page to appear when you start Netscape. Many people like their first screen to be a search engine, such as Yahoo! <http://www.yahoo.com>. The Netscape Help button or the Yahoo! Help button will show you how to change your start-up page. (For more customization, see your browser's Preferences section, on the View menu.)

There are several ways to access a **Web page** using Netscape. One option is to follow a **hyperlink,** which can be either text or an image. Textual hyperlinks, or **hypertext,** have a different look from the rest of the text. Depending on the browser you use, hypertext will be either a different color or underlined, or both. To follow a link, use your mouse to drag the arrow over the hypertext. When positioned over a link, the arrow will turn into a hand. Click the mouse, and you will go to that Web page. (Some links on some pages are not marked, but whenever your cursor arrow turns into a hand, you can click there and be taken somewhere else.)

Another option to clicking a link is to type out a page's address (the URL or uniform resource locator). Click on the Open button on the toolbar, type the URL in the box provided, and press Return. To navigate through a sequence of pages you have already seen, use the Back and Forward buttons on the toolbar. You may also access a Web page you have already seen by choosing it from your list of **Bookmarks,** from entries on the History list (from the Window menu), or from the Go menu.

(*Note:* URLs in this book, within the text, are enclosed in angle brackets, < >, for readability. The angle brackets are not part of the address.)

QUICK VIEW
How Can I Use Text-Only Access to the Internet?

Some students have access to computers that will give them only text from the Internet. If your computer gives you access to Lynx or some other text-only browser, this page will help you get off to a fast start. Otherwise, please turn to page 5 for more detailed instructions.

Using Lynx and Other Text-Only Browsers

Lynx is the most popular text-only browser. With text-only browsers, you cannot view the multimedia functions on the Web, such as pictures, audio, or video. You see only text. (*Note:* You do not need TCP/IP software, see page 5, to use Lynx.)

If you have a computer account at school, find out if it is a **UNIX** or VMS account. Chances are it will be a UNIX account. (Lynx runs on both, but our example shows how it works on UNIX.) Next, find out whether Lynx is available; if so, you can access Lynx by logging on to your computer account and then on to Lynx. After logging on, you will see either a $ or a %. Then type lynx. Your screen will look like this:

```
$ lynx
```

The first screen displayed should be a page containing information about the World Wide Web and giving you access to other pages.

To access a specific Web page, type lynx followed by the specific Web page's Internet address (its URL). For example, if you wanted to go to Netscape's home page, your command line would look like this:

```
$ lynx http://www.home.netscape.com
```

When you view a Web page, the hypertext links (shortcuts to other pages) will appear in bold. To move your cursor to a link (in bold text), use your up and down arrow keys. When you place your cursor on the bold text, the text will become highlighted. To follow the link, press the right-arrow key. To go back, press the left-arrow key.

At the bottom of the screen, you will find a list of other commands. Simply type the first letter in the command name to execute that command. When you are finished, type q to quit. You will be asked if you really want to quit; type y for yes. This will bring you back to your system prompt (the $ or the %).

(*Note:* URLs in this book, within the text, are enclosed in angle brackets, < >, for readability. The angle brackets are not part of the address.)

CHAPTER ONE
FINDING INFORMATION ON THE INTERNET

The Internet started in the 1960s as a project by the U.S. government to link supercomputers; eventually, its networking technology also came to be used by academic institutions. In the beginning, the Internet was "user hostile," and the numbers of computers and people it connected were limited. With the creation of the World Wide Web in the early 1990s by Tim Berners-Lee in Switzerland, the Internet became much more "user friendly." Today, the Internet, a global network of computers, has a great many parts: the World Wide Web, Usenet, Gopher, Telnet, and FTP (file transfer protocol).

Technically, the World Wide Web is an Internet facility that uses hypertext to link multimedia sources. Web **servers** store files that can be viewed or downloaded with a Web **browser** via **HTTP (hypertext transfer protocol)**. The most popular text-only browser is Lynx; some popular graphic browsers are Netscape, Explorer, and AOL (America Online). This book's examples use Netscape; Explorer works much the same way as Netscape.

How the Internet Works—In Brief

To find the information you want, you should know a little about how your computer works with the Internet. That is the subject of the next five brief sections. If you are not interested in learning more about how computers work, you can skip to "How to Find the Information You Want," on page 8.

Hardware and Software
To gain access to the Internet, you need a computer with the appropriate hardware and software and an **ISP (Internet service provider)**. Some popular ISPs are AOL, CompuServe, MSN, and AT&T WorldNet. To access the Internet from home, you need a computer with a **modem** to connect your computer to the phone lines. Most modems run at 28.8K or 56K **bps (bits per second)**. Faster modems can save you money if you are charged by the amount of time you spend on the Web. You will need a computer that has at least 16MB **(megabytes)** of **RAM (random-access memory)**. (*Note:* You will also need to find out the networking capabilities of your ISP; information is transferred only as fast as your ISP's slowest connection.)

For software, you will need **TCP/IP (transmission control protocol/ Internet protocol**—languages that allow computers to communicate with each other) to provide an interface between your computer and the Internet. If you have a Macintosh, you need MacTCP. If you have an IBM or clone, you need Winsock (which stands for "Windows socket"). Generally these networking protocol utilities are already provided with your computer system. There are two main types of browsers, graphic and text-only, which are explained in more detail on pages 3 and 4.

Client/Server Systems

The Web works on a client/server system. The **client** is your computer and software; a server is any computer that houses files (text, audio, video, software) you want; and **networks** are systems that connect clients and servers. Think of your computer (the client) as a customer in a restaurant and the information provider (the server) as the chef. You order a meal (the information), and the waiter or waitress (the network) brings it back to you (your computer).

URLs and How They Work

To access a file by means of a Web browser, you must know the file's location. A **URL (uniform resource locator)**, the Internet address for a file, is composed as follows:

```
protocol://server and domain name/file path/file
```

For example, suppose a student named Jane Smith at the University of Tennessee, Knoxville, has created a personal Web page for her résumé. The address for that page might be as follows:

```
http://funnelweb.utcc.utk.edu/~jSmith/Resume.html
```

Here, http is the **protocol**; funnelweb.utcc.utk.edu is the server and **domain name**; ~jSmith is the **file path**; and Resume.html is the file. When you type this address in Netscape or Lynx, the browser reads the URL's components to find the specific page. The first part of the URL not only tells you what type of file you are accessing, but it also tells the computer what kind of language it needs to speak. In this case, you want a Web page in **HTML (hypertext mark-up language)**, so the computer needs to speak hypertext, using HTTP (hypertext transfer protocol).

The next thing your computer needs to know is where the file is kept. This is what the second part of the URL, the server and domain name, designates. The server where the Web page in this example is kept is called funnelweb. The funnelweb server is a computer at the University of Tennessee, Knoxville (UTK), that is denoted by utcc.utk.edu. The .edu tells you that the domain is "educational." Other types of domains are .com for "commercial"; .mil for "military"; .org for "organizational"; .net for "network"; and .gov for "governmental" sites. Recently, seven new domain categories were added: .firm for "business"; .store for "retail"; `.nom` for "individual"; `.rec` for "recreational"; `.info` for "informational"; `.arts` for "cultural"; and `.web` for "Web-oriented" sites.

Of all the Web pages at UTK, how does your computer know which one is Jane Smith's? The last two parts of the URL tell how to get to Jane Smith's file. (Note the tilde symbol [~], which is generally used to indicate a personal page.) The user identification for Jane's file path, or "user area," is `~jSmith`. The file your computer wants is `Resume.html`. Now that the computer knows where to go, which file to get, and how to read it, the computer can display Jane Smith's page on your browser's screen (such as Netscape or Lynx). Notice that the file name has a mix of upper- and lowercase letters. Most URLs are case sensitive, so be sure to enter the URL exactly, including the uppercase letters. Note also that URLs never contain spaces.

Downloading Information

When you access a page, it sometimes takes a long time for the page to appear on your screen. If you are using Netscape and look at the bottom of the browser window while waiting for a Web page to appear, you should see a display indicating the percentage of the amount of data transferred. When you access a Web page, a copy of the file is transferred to your computer's memory. This is called **downloading** a file. So, when you are **surfing** the Web, copies of all those Web pages are downloaded to your computer. However, the file is not downloaded all at once; it is transferred in pieces, or **packets.** Depending on the size of the files you are downloading, the length of time it takes for the Web page to appear will vary: A large Web page or a Web page with lots of graphics will slow the transfer. Image files are larger than text files and take longer to download. To shorten the download time in Netscape, turn off Auto Load Images (from the Preferences menu under "View"). Also turn off **Java** loading. To remove the check mark, click on Auto Load Images. To turn Auto Load Images back on, simply click on that line and it will be reactivated. By turning off Images, Web pages containing graphics will download faster, but you will not see any of the graphics automatically. To see the graphics individually, you have to click on each picture frame; to see all the graphics at once, turn Auto Load Images back on and click on Reload (from the View menu) or on the Reload button on the toolbar. Your computer stores Web pages it has loaded in its **cache;** some computers empty their cache automatically, while with others you may need to empty it yourself.

Internet Service Providers

To get onto the Internet, you will need an ISP. Before looking into commercial ISPs, check with your college or university's computing center because some schools offer Internet services for home access to students, faculty, and staff. Internet services through your school will probably be the best deal. Although your school may not always have the latest upgrades of hardware or software, the price will probably be hard to beat.

If you decide to go with a commercial ISP, you should do some comparison shopping. Think about what you will be using your Internet connection for, such as e-mail, Internet mail, graphic access to the Web, file transfer, Telnet, or storing Web pages. Once you decide what you will need, find out which ISPs offer all those services. After you have gathered a list of possible providers, ask some questions:

- What is the level of customer support, such as online help, user manuals, and telephone support (preferably 24 hours)?
- Is there an installation fee?
- Is there an extra cost for e-mail? If so, is the charge by message, by time, or by size of the message? Is there a storage fee for mail?
- Are there different rates for access at different times of the day?
- Is there a local dial-in number? Will long-distance fees be charged?
- What is the **bandwidth** (the amount of information that can be transferred across a network at one time)? The size of the bandwidth can affect access speed.
- Is all the necessary software provided, such as TCP/IP and a browser (such as Netscape or Explorer)?
- Is storage space available for Web pages? If so, what is the charge?
- Are backup servers available to help maintain continuous access?
- What kind of security is offered?
- Read some reviews, such as those from *PC Week* (also available on the Web).

How to Find the Information You Want

The Internet is a vast and rapidly changing conglomeration of information. Finding your way to the particular piece of information you need can be difficult if you are not familiar with the search options available.

World Wide Web Search Engines
You can search the Web with **search engines** such as Yahoo! or AltaVista; search FTP archives with **Archie** and **ArchiePlex**; burrow through **Gopher** with **Veronica**, Archie, **Jughead**, and Gopher Jewels; and access library computers directly with Hytelnet <http://www.lights.com/hytelnet>.

A Note on the URLs in This Book

Change is inherent in the Web. As we prepared this guide, we verified every URL we list. But, by the time you read this book, some of the URLs will almost certainly have changed. If you cannot find one of these URLs, try deleting the last set of letters in the URL (going "up" a level in the address). If that does not work, try searching for the page's title in your favorite search engine, such as Yahoo! or AltaVista.

Sometimes the problem is *not finding enough information;* more often the problem is *finding way too much information;* and, always, the problem is *finding the right information.* Here are some suggestions for solving these problems.

Search engines are computer programs that allow you to find the information you want through key word searches. The search engine provides a text box, into which you type key words associated with the information you want. Most search engines also offer more complex searches involving some variation of **Boolean logic** with the aid of "logical operators," such as AND, OR, and NOT. (Some search engines let "+" stand for AND and "–" stand for NOT.) Some even offer more advanced searching, such as limiting your search to specific dates, ranking key words in order of appearance within the document, or giving you other ways to refine your search.

There are hundreds of search engines for the Internet—too many to discuss here. Two popular and different types of search engines, Yahoo! (a searchable, browsable directory) and AltaVista (a powerful search engine), are briefly described below. For a more extensive list of search engines, see the Library of Congress list at <http://lcweb.loc.gov/global/search.html>.

Yahoo! <http://www.yahoo.com>. Yahoo! is both a search engine and a directory made of subject trees. A **subject tree** is a hierarchical index system for finding information. You begin with a general subject, such as Medicine, and follow the subject tree's branches to a specific document. Yahoo!'s subject trees begin on its main page, which can be found at its URL.

Yahoo! is a good way to start searching because it looks at only a few key elements. Consequently, Yahoo! is the place to go for general discussions of your topic. To learn more about how to do a search on Yahoo!, click on the Options link located by the text box where you type in your key words.

AltaVista <http://www.altavista.com>. Unlike Yahoo!, AltaVista does a thorough full-text search of documents for key words. If you put a fairly general key word into AltaVista, you will most likely receive hundreds or even thousands of links to pages that may only mention your topic in passing. AltaVista is a good place to search for obscure items or for very specific topics.

If you are getting too many hits for a topic on AltaVista, try doing the same search on Yahoo!; this should cut down the number of possible matches. Likewise, if you are searching on Yahoo! and you are not getting enough matches, try AltaVista.

AltaVista offers both a Simple Search and an Advanced Search. The Advanced Search helps you limit your results by specifying date ranges and ranking key words. To find out more about Simple and Advanced Searches on AltaVista, click the Help button at the top of the first AltaVista page.

Metasearch engines. Today there are a number of metasearch engines—search engines that search a number of other search engines at one time. For example, on Dogpile (<http://www.dogpile.com>), instead of getting a result such as "15 hits found," you may read "5 hits on Yahoo!; 10 hits on AltaVista; 12 hits on InfoSeek," etc. Then you can choose which results you may want to look at. This feature is often a great timesaver. Interestingly, however, the same search that may turn up 15 hits on AltaVista if you use a metasearch engine, may turn up 25 hits if you search on AltaVista alone. As a consequence, while some people prefer metasearch engines, others (including this book's authors) prefer to use one or two or three separate search engines consistently. (Other metasearch engines are listed at <http://www.islandnet.com/~pb/frames.html>.)

Searching via Key Words
Key word searches may require some imagination if you are not getting the results you hoped for. In most cases, your search was either too narrow or too broad. The tips below should help. Also, when you do find information you want, remember to check it for credibility. (See pages 16–18 on how to judge the reliability of Internet information.)

Narrowing a search. If you are getting too many **hits** (successful key word matches), try narrowing your search by adding more key words. Sometimes this will help, because most search engines will look for each of the words independently but display the pages with the most matches first. Usually, you can narrow your search and make sure that all the key words appear in the document by using AND between the key words.

⌐🖰 *Info Bit*—Narrow your search by looking for the most current information (or for the most relevant dates) in the AltaVista Advanced Search by entering a starting and an ending date for the information.

✒ *Info Bit*—Some search engines, such as Yahoo!, allow you to search within document titles only. This will narrow your search results and may give you better sources on your topic.

Broadening a search. If you are not getting enough hits, you need to broaden your search by deleting some of the more specific key words or substituting synonyms for the key words you already have listed. For example, for a search about how to make a Web page, you might try several search strings, such as "Web page design," "creating a Web page," and "making a Web page." Also, you may want to try a more general category under which your topic falls. For example, if you want information on the Hopi god Kokopeli, but you get only one or two hits, you could try searching for "Hopi religion" or just "Hopi."

✒ *Info Bit*—The Web is a big place with millions of documents, and it is growing by the hour. No single search engine can cover the whole Web. Each search engine covers different, although overlapping, territory. If your search does not work with the first engine you use, try running it on several different ones, or try a metasearch engine.

✒ *Info Bit*—Some search engines are designed to find specific topics, such as Law Crawler at <http://www.lawcrawler.com> or the Amazing Environmental Organization Web Directory at <http://www. webdirectory.com>.

Finding phrases. If you want to find documents containing a specific phrase, such as "Green Bay Packers," put the phrase in double quotation marks to lock them together. Otherwise you will get thousands of pages that have only "green" or "bay" or "packers" in them.

Searching via Subject Trees

As described previously in the section on Yahoo!, a subject tree is a hierarchical index of topics that allows you to begin with a broad category and follow the subject tree's branches down to a specific file. Subject trees can be good places to start your search because you can get an idea of the different types of information available on your topic.

One of the first and best subject trees is The Virtual Library <http://www.w3.org/vl>. There are different ways to search The Virtual Library. You can start searching the Subject Index on the main page, or you can search the Category Subtree or the Top Ten Most Popular Fields.

Other Places to Start

You can start your Web research in many places besides search engines. One possibility is traditional reference tools (such as encyclopedias) that

⌐🖰 *Info Byte: Some Common Error Messages*

Connection refused by server

Server is busy. The maximum number of simultaneous connections has probably been reached. Try again later.

Document contains no data

First, try clicking the link again. If this doesn't work, there may be a glitch in the network.

Forbidden access (Error 401)

For some reason, the creator or maintainer of a page does not want any "outside" visitors, and he or she has restricted the access to the page.

No DNS entry

Means "No Domain Name System," or that the server does not exist. If you are linking to a page from another, try clicking the link again. If you are entering the URL, make sure you have entered it correctly— with any capital letters and without spaces. If the URL is correct, the server may not be working.

Not found (Error 404)

The file you are looking for is not on this server. It may have been moved or deleted.

No response

There may be too many connections, or the server may be down for some reason. Try again later.

Transfer interrupted!

For some reason, the server was not able to transfer all of the data for this page. Try reloading.

Error 400

Your request could not be understood by the server. Your Web browser may be malfunctioning or your Internet connection may be unreliable. Try shutting down and restarting your computer.

are increasingly available on the Web. For example, *Encyclopaedia Britannica* is now available online, free, at <http://www.britannica.com>. Many teachers believe the best way to begin a research project is to consult such traditional reference tools; more and more of these are available on the Web.

Another possible place to start your Web research is to think about what kind of place might be likely to have information on your subject, and look for that place's Web site. For example, if you're researching a medical topic, why not start at the National Institutes of Health's home page (<http://www. nih.gov/>)? If you're writing about the FBI, remember to look at the FBI's own site (<http://www.fbi.gov/>). If you're writing about any kind of historical topic, from the Dead Sea Scrolls to the Civil War, why not start at the Smithsonian (<http://www.si.edu/>)? Giving a few minutes' thought to what kind of place would be likely to have good information on your topic, and to finding and checking that place's Web site, can pay big dividends in research success. You can also try library search engines, especially the Library of Congress (<http://www.lcweb.loc.gov/>). (Be aware that library search engines often operate under a tighter set of search rules than Internet search engines, so if the key word you have chosen to use on a library search engine is not retrieving the kinds of sources you are looking for, you may need to try other key words or get help from a librarian.)

Other Protocols: Telnet and Gopher

Web servers communicate through HTTP (hypertext transfer protocol), but there are other, older information systems, such as Telnet and Gopher, that communicate through other protocols. The URLs for these other Internet systems begin with a different protocol abbreviation, or prompt, such as `telnet://`, `gopher://`, or `ftp://`. Telnet and Gopher are described here; FTP (file transfer protocol) is discussed in Chapter Three.

Telnet. Some electronic **bulletin boards,** library catalogs, and school computer accounts are not part of the Web. To access these sources, you can use **Telnet,** a protocol that lets you communicate with computers that use the UNIX operating system. To use Telnet, you need to log on to another computer (a remote host). When you log on, a text-only screen identical to the screen of the remote host will appear. Then you can issue commands from your computer and have them carried out by the remote host.

A Telnet session's first screen usually lists instructions for logging on, accessing the Help page, and logging off. If you get a blank screen, try pressing Enter (or Return). If you get a screen with instructions, *read it carefully,* because when you want to exit a session, you may not remember how. If no instructions are given, try typing ? and pressing Enter to get the

Help page. To exit, hold the Command key and type q if you are using a Macintosh, or hold the Control key and type q if you are using a PC.

To use Telnet, you will need Telnet software. If your ISP does not provide the software, you can download it from the Internet for free. For a Macintosh, get Better Telnet at <http://www.cstone.net/~rbraun/mac/telnet/>. For a PC, get EWAN Telnet from <http://www.iconn.iphil.net/services/telnet.html>.

Gopher. Gopher is a menu-driven information system started at the University of Minnesota and named after its mascot, the "Gophers." It is a predecessor of the World Wide Web. However, Gopher menu systems and files can be accessed via the Web. There is a lot of good information on Gopher that is not available elswhere on the Internet. If you want to search Gopher, a good place to start is with Gopher Jewels at <http://www.uccs.edu/gopher/jewels.html>. Gopher Jewels catalogs many Gopher sites by subject tree. For a more thorough search of Gopher sites, use a search engine, such as Jughead (document title search) or Veronica (full-text search). For more on Gopher, Veronica, and Jughead, go to <http://lcweb.loc.gov/loc/guides/navigate.html>.

Integrating Research Sources
While the focus of this book is the World Wide Web, with particular attention to doing research on the Web and correctly citing your Web sources in your research papers, it needs to be pointed out that few college teachers today will accept papers that use *only* Web-based research, and some teachers frown on using *any* Web-based research. Thus, even if you are in a situation where Web research is acceptable, chances are you will need to integrate your Web research with information from traditional print sources as well. Here are two ways to go about integrating your research sources, accompanied by "road maps" to help you visualize each process.

Past-Present-Future (or General to Specific). A traditional approach to library research would suggest starting with reference tools (such as encyclopedias), moving on to books (by way of the *Library of Congress Subject Headings* list), and then going to periodical publications (via periodical indexes). Finally, with a wealth of background information in hand, you could go on to collect firsthand information—from interviews, direct observation, surveys, laboratory tests, or fieldwork. Within this structure, shown in Road Map One, the *last* step would be to do Web-based research, perhaps using as search terms in Yahoo! and AltaVista the key words (including author's names) gathered from all the earlier research steps. This

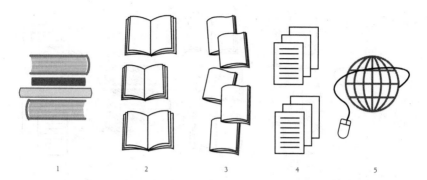

Road Map One: 1 = *reference tools;* 2 = *books;* 3 = *periodical articles;*
4 = *primary research;* 5 = *Web-based research*

method starts slowly but hardly ever fails to produce rich results. The downside is that it starts so slowly and the early stages are not much fun; consequently, some students tend to put off starting until it really is too late for this rather deliberate process to work. The upside is that given enough time and effort, the process just about always works.

Start Hot, Finish Strong. Few people who become accustomed to doing research on the Web can resist the temptation to at least try their topic in a few search engines before they do anything else. Suppose you are writing about "the role of sign language interpreters in the CIA"— why not try that phrase, and a few variations of it, in your favorite search engines before you do anything else? If you get some good hits, you can still proceed backward through the previous pattern (roughly, Web materials, then print periodical articles, then books, then reference tools, then firsthand research), working from leads in Web-based sources (authors' names, possible bibliographical information) through increasingly broader (and, usually, older) sources. This method is shown in Road Map Two.

Two cautions go with this method: First, if you do not find good Web sources in the first step, you probably need to use the Past-Present-Future method instead. Second, no matter how good the Web sources you may find in the first step are, you *must still* do the other steps, and do them carefully and thoroughly. Otherwise, you will risk writing a paper that is shallow and one-dimensional, and, because you are relying too much on few sources of only one kind, the possibility of accidental plagiarism is strong. The weak

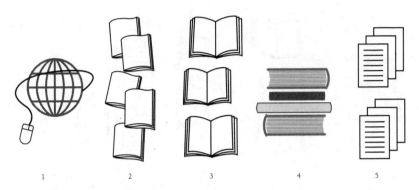

1   2   3   4   5

Road Map Two: *1 = Web-based research; 2 = periodical articles; 3 = books;*
4 = reference sources; 5 = primary research

side of this process is that some students are tempted to stop after the first
step. The strong side is that if you do get some good hits early on, that rush
of initial success can carry you forward pretty far into the process.

How to Judge the Reliability of Internet Information

Students who are accustomed to doing research in libraries face new issues
when they start doing research on the Internet. Before a book or journal
appears in a university library, it has usually gone through a number of
checks to make sure the information in it is reliable. For example, if you
find a copy of *Moby Dick* in your university library, you can be sure you
are getting a generally accepted version of the real thing. But if you find a
copy of *Moby Dick* on the Internet, you need to give some thought to *where
you found it,* whether the person who put it on the Internet is *a reliable
authority on the subject* (someone who can be trusted not to enter his or her
own personal, political, or scholarly biases into the text), and whether your
professor will *accept your judgment* of the reliability of that material.

   Arguably, student researchers should always make these decisions,
even about materials they find in the university library. However, judging
the reliability of sources found on the Internet is crucial because there
is no regulating body that monitors the reliability of what is on the
Internet. Although there is so much information on the Internet that it
can seem like a university library, it is actually more like a huge open-air
market. In one corner there might be reliable sources from whom you
can obtain valuable information. But over in another corner there might

be weirdos, whackos, and eccentrics, from whom anything you obtain is, at best, questionable. The problem is that on the Internet there is no way to tell the difference. Someone who wants to turn *Moby Dick* into a glorification of bloodsports or an animal rights tract can post a rewritten version with no indication of its differences from Melville's original. There's a saying in Latin, *caveat emptor,* or "let the buyer beware." When it comes to doing your research on the Internet, the saying should be *caveat internauta,* or "let the surfer beware."

Here is a list of points to consider when you are trying to judge the reliability of information you find on the Internet:

- **Who is the author or sponsor of the page?** On the page you are citing, or on a page linked to it, that individual or organization should be identified, that individual's qualifications should be apparent, and other avenues of verification should be open to you. For a good example of a reliable source, see "Notes about this document" for the hypertext version of *Pride and Prejudice* at <http://www.pemberley.com/janeinfo/ pridprej.html>. A page created by a person or an organization that does not provide this information is *not* a good source to cite. (You can often find out more about a page's source by deleting the last section of its URL and Reloading your browser, thus moving up a level in the Web site's hierarchy.)

- **Are there obvious reasons for bias?** If the page is presented by a tobacco company consortium, you should be suspicious of its reports on the addictiveness of nicotine. Is there any advertising? If the page is sponsored by Acme Track Shoes, you should be suspicious of its claims for Acme track shoes' performance.

- **Is contact information provided?** If the only identification available is something cryptic, such as "Society for Feruginous Retorts," be suspicious of the page's reliability. If the page is sponsored by a reputable person or organization, there should be some other way to verify that reputation, such as an e-mail or a postal address. (Note that a tilde [~] in the page's address usually indicates a personal home page and may require more searching for reliability.)

- **Is there a copyright symbol on the page?** If so, who holds the copyright?

- **Is this page a "zombie,"** or one considered "walking dead" because the person who posted it no longer maintains or updates it? Even though the information is "alive" in that it is still accessible, it is "dead" in that it may no longer be accurate. Look for a last-updated date if your topic requires current information.

- **What is the purpose of the page?** Why is this information being posted—as information, as a public service, as news, as a research tool for academics, as a personal ax to grind, or as a way to gain attention?

- **How well organized is the page?** Is the page easy to navigate? Is it complete? How credible are the links it provides?

- **Is the information on the page *primary* or *secondary*?** That is, is it a report of facts, such as a medical researcher's article counting cases of "mad cow" disease in England, thus making it primary information, or is it an Internet newsgroup discussion about "mad cow" disease, thus making it secondary information? The papers and reports you write for your college classes need to be based on primary information whenever possible. The further away from the primary sources your own sources are, the less reliable the information may be.

- **Can you verify the information** on the Web page some other way? For example, can you check the page's bibliography (if there is one) against your library's holdings or check the information against a source in the library?

- **If you are worried that the information may lack credibility, try starting with a source you know is reputable.** For example, if you have to do a project on the latest in cancer research, you can begin your search at major cancer research institutes, such as the Mayo Clinic in Rochester, Minnesota <http://www.mayo.edu>.

- Finally, remember that **even though a page might not meet your standards as a citable source, it may provide good ideas** or point to other usable sources. Also, be sure not to stop your search at the first page you find—shop around and do some comparing so that you can have points of reference.

Ultimately, the problem with reliability of information on the Web is like the whispering game children play. Someone whispers a message to the first child, who whispers it to the second, and so on. By the time it gets to the last child, the message is hopelessly distorted. Web pages can work the same way when people get their information from other people's Web pages: The first person who posts information may make a few small errors, the second unintentionally repeats them and makes one or two more, the third makes a few more, and so on. For information seekers it can be impossible to tell where in the chain the information is coming from, but that makes a difference in the information's reliability. So it is always a good idea to check against a library reference.

CHAPTER TWO
HOW TO DOCUMENT INFORMATION
FROM ELECTRONIC SOURCES

Whenever you are doing research and writing for a classroom assignment, documenting your sources correctly is important. If the information, ideas, or other kinds of materials (such as drawings and graphics) in your paper are from a source, you need to let your readers know by adding appropriate documentation. (And if you quote passages, you need to add quotation marks or make block quotations as well.) The documentation you provide needs to be complete enough that a reader who wants to check your sources will be able to find them. Material borrowed from the Internet and other electronic sources, just like print sources, must be properly documented. This chart compares the elements of documentation for print sources with those of documentation for electronic sources.

Books	Articles	Electronic Sources
Full name of author or editor	Full name of author	Full name of author (if available)
Exact title	Exact title	Exact title
Place of publication and publisher	Journal name	Type of source (Web page, FTP site, online journal, CD-ROM, etc.)
	Volume and issue (if pages are numbered consecutively throughout the volume, you can omit issue number)	
Year of publication	Year of publication	Date accessed
Page numbers	Page numbers	URL (if appropriate)

Portable versus Online Sources

There are two kinds of electronic sources of information—*unchangeable* and *changeable*—and they need to be documented in slightly different ways.

Portable (or Unchangeable) Sources
Suppose you look up material on a **CD-ROM (compact disc, read-only memory),** such as InfoTrac, Encarta, or some other portable database. As an electronic source, the CD-ROM is stable—that is, anyone could look at it today, next month, or next year, and find the same information. It has a date and place of publication (although here "publication" actually means "production") and a version number, which should be shown in your documentation just as they would be for a journal article. Thus, for unchangeable sources there is no need to add extra elements to your documentation.

Online (or Changeable) Sources
For materials you find on the Internet, you need to add some information to your documentation. Usually, it includes the date you accessed the information and its URL. Sometimes, you may be required to include the path you took to get to the page or even a hard copy (a printout) of the page. If information you find on the Internet is crucial to your work, it is always a good idea to print out a hard copy, just in case.

Different Styles for Different Fields

If you are taking a sociology class, your teacher may require you to use the American Psychological Association (APA) style, which is also what academics in the social sciences, such as psychology or education, generally use. English or composition classes use Modern Language Association (MLA) style, which is what literature and language specialists use. When documenting Web and Internet sources, many teachers of first-year students recommend the Alliance for Computers and Writing (ACW) style <http://english.ttu.edu/acw>. Professors for higher-level classes or classes in other fields may expect you to use some other style—the Council of Biology Editors (CBE) style used in the life sciences; the *Chicago Manual of Style* (CMS) superscript style used in business, history, and many hard sciences; or even the Institute of Electrical and Electronics Engineers (IEEE) style <http://www.ieee.org> used in fields such as computer science. Although there are hundreds of different styles, the right one for you will probably look close to one of the four varieties presented here.

When and What to Document

Here are seven simple guidelines to help you decide when and what to document:

1. If you use the exact language of your source, you must use quotation marks, or set the quote off as a block, and cite the source.

2. If you put the source's information into your own words (creating a paraphrase), you *still* must cite your source.

3. Use direct quotations only if there is something unique about your source's language or if your own words will not do the job better.

4. Directly quote only as much as you need—the bare minimum.

5. If you use information that is not common knowledge, you must cite the source. If this information would not be familiar to someone who had not researched the subject, it is not common knowledge and its source must be cited.

6. Cite all kinds of sources, not just words and facts. Sources can also include drawings, photos, artwork, ideas, music—anything you use that is not yours.

7. To work your quoted or otherwise borrowed material into the text more smoothly, introduce it with the name of the source. To introduce your borrowed material, use a tag line—for example, "As Dr. Stanley Prusiner, one of the leading authorities on prion diseases, said. . . ."

QUICK VIEW
AMERICAN PSYCHOLOGICAL ASSOCIATION (APA)
AUTHOR-DATE STYLE

APA style places the author's name and date of publication within parentheses in the text, linked to a list of references (titled *References*) at the end of the document. Although the focus of this guide is electronic sources, here is a brief overview of APA documentation style. For more information, consult the *Publication Manual of the American Psychological Association*, 4th edition (1994).

Citations in the Text
Citations in the text generally include the author's last name and the year in parentheses. So a citation to something by Bill Jones in 1988 would be (Jones, 1988). The parenthetical citation precedes the sentence's final punctuation. If the author's name has already appeared in the sentence, the year of publication follows it in parentheses. APA requires page numbers only if you are citing a direct quotation or a specific table, figure, or equation. If you need to include page numbers (and some teachers want page numbers for everything), use *p.* or *pp.*

Parenthetical citations for direct quotations in the text appear after the closing quotation marks but before the final punctuation. If the quotation is more than forty words long, it should be indented an inch. If the quotation is set off, the citation appears after the quotation's final punctuation.

Entries in the References List
Each entry in the reference list must match a citation, and the entire list must be double spaced. The entries should be alphabetized by the author's last name and, in the case of multiple entries by the same authors, chronologically, beginning with the earliest. APA recommends that the first line of every entry should be indented and subsequent lines be flush left. Each entry has four elements: author, date, title, and publication information. A typical entry for a book looks like this:

> Schultz, E., & Lavenda, R. (1998) <u>Cultural anthropology: Perspectives on the human condition</u> (2nd ed.). Mountain View, CA: Mayfield.

Note: We show APA references here with paragraph-style indents; some teachers may prefer "hanging" indents (first line flush left, subsequent lines indented). According to the FAQ on the APA Web site, either style may be acceptable.

APA Style for Citing Electronic Sources

The basic citation has five elements: author, date, title, document type, and publication information. The information here has been supplemented by APA's Web page, "Electronic Reference Formats Recommended by the American Psychological Association" <http://www.apa.org/journals/webref.html>.

CD-ROMs and Other Portable Databases

If you use information from a CD-ROM or other unchangeable source (such as a magnetic tape or commercially produced disk), you need to name the author, date, and title just as for a print source. Next, specify the date accessed and the nature of the electronic medium. At the end of the entry, give the name and source location of the producer. A typical entry looks like this (because there is no author in this example, the publication's name comes first):

> The world factbook 1994. (1994). Washington, DC:
> Central Intelligence Agency. Retrieved Oct. 10,
> 1996, from CD-ROM.

You may encounter a CD-ROM version of a document that is also available in hard copy. If so, your citation needs to include information for both (while making it clear that you accessed the CD-ROM version). This note is for an abstract that was read on CD-ROM:

> Morring, F., Jr. (1994, May 16). Russian
> hardware allows earlier station experiments
> [Abstract]. Aviation Week & Space Technology, 140,
> 57. Retrieved Oct. 10, 1996 from CD-ROM: InfoTrac
> General Periodicals Index-A: Abstract 15482317.

Online Sources

For changeable sources, use this format: author's name, date of the most recent revision (if available), title of the source, date of access, and identification of the type of document (such as online serial or personal home page). In place of a publisher is the complete URL. If the URL will not fit on one line, break it after a period or slash. Here is an example:

> Land, T. (1996, March 31). Web extension to
> American Psychological Association style (WEAPAS)
> [online] (Rev. 1.2.4). URL retrieved April 24,
> 1997 from the World Wide Web:
> http://www.beadslands.com/weapas/.

QUICK VIEW
COUNCIL OF BIOLOGY EDITORS (CBE)
CITATION-SEQUENCE SYSTEM

The CBE style manual presents two systems of documentation. The one summarized here uses numbers in the text that refer to a numbered list of references at the end of the document. Because our purpose here is to show how CBE treats electronic sources, we summarize only the citation sequence system. For full details, refer to *Scientific Style and Format: The CBE Manual for Authors, Editors, and Publishers*, 6th edition (1994).

Citations in the Text
When a source is first used in the text, it is assigned a number that it retains whenever it is used again. The number appears in superscript immediately after the source is referred to, not separated by a space. If more than one source is cited, the numbers are separated by commas without spaces. Here is a typical entry (taken from Leslie C. Perelman, James Paradis, and Edward Barrett, *The Mayfield Handbook of Technical and Scientific Writing*, 1998):

> The oncogene jun has presently become one of
> the best-known oncogenes because of its ability to
> act as a transcription factor[1]. One study[2] examined
> . . . .

Entries in the References List
Titled *References* or *Cited References*, the whole list is double spaced. The sequence is established by the order in which the items appear in the text. The number of the entry is flush left and is followed by a period. Each entry has four basic elements: author, title, publication information, and page numbers. Authors' first and middle names are abbreviated, as are other elements; the abbreviations are not followed by periods. Here is an example of a journal article entry:

> 1. Lenski RE, May RM. The evolution of virulence
> in parasites and pathogens: reconciliation
> between two competing hypotheses. J Theoret
> Biol 1994;169:253-65.

Here is a typical entry for a book:

> 13. Mandelbrot BB. The fractal geometry of

nature.

San Francisco: WH Freeman; 1995. 460 p.

CBE Style for Citing Electronic Sources

The CBE style for citing electronic sources is still evolving. The pattern for online sources recommended here is taken from *The Mayfield Handbook of Technical and Scientific Writing,* and is consistent with other CBE formats.

CD-ROMs and Other Portable Databases

For unchangeable sources, the author, date, and title information is provided just as for a print source. In brackets after the title, identify the medium. At the end of the entry, include the name of the database and its location. Here is a typical entry:

9. Morring F Jr. Russian hardware allows earlier station experiments [CD-ROM]. Aviat Wk Space Technol 1994;140:57. Abstract from: InfoTrac General Periodicals Index-A: Abstract 15482317.

Online Sources

The *CBE Manual* does not require the full Internet address for changeable sources. Nonetheless, it makes sense to include this additional information. Here is a sample entry with the type of document provided and the URL and date of access added:

1. Brooker MIH, Slee AV. New taxa and some new nomenclature in *Eucalyptus*. Muelleria [abstract online] 1996; 9(75-85). Available from WWW; <http://155.187.10.12/cpbrpublications/ brooker-slee2.html> (Accessed 1997 Feb 13).

QUICK VIEW
CHICAGO MANUAL OF STYLE (CMS) SUPERSCRIPT SYSTEM

Three documentation systems are presented in *The Chicago Manual of Style,* 14th edition (1993). The one shown here uses superscript numbers keyed to numbered endnotes or footnotes. It is based on an adaptation of CMS style for college writers: *A Manual for Writers of Term Papers, Theses, and Dissertations,* 6th edition (1996), by Kate Turabian. In the FAQ on their Web page, the editors of *Chicago* recommend Turabian for writers whose manuscripts will *not* be published as books.

Citations in the Text
Note numbers that appear in the text are superscript numbers. They normally go at the end of the sentence, following the final punctuation; if they must be used within a sentence, they should go after a punctuation mark. CMS superscript notations in the text will look like this:

One literary critic notes "Austen's uncertainty about the inner life of Darcy,"[1] and another explains that Austen's novels, like those of many other nineteenth-century British authors, empower their heroines "over their own plot" and place them at the center of the action.[2]

If you use a direct quotation in the text, the note number appears after the closing quotation mark. A direct quotation that is eight lines or more should be set off, single spaced, and indented four spaces. The note number appears right after the quotation's final punctuation.

Entries in the Notes List
Each entry in the list of notes should correspond to a superscript number in the text. The entries are arranged numerically, with the reference number followed by a period and a space. The entire list of notes should be double spaced, with the first line of each entry indented half an inch.

Each entry generally has four elements: author, title, publication information, and page numbers. The author's name is given in normal order (first name, then last name). Here is a basic entry for a book:

2. Hilary M. Lips, <u>Sex and Gender: An Introduction,</u> 3rd ed. (Mountain View, CA: Mayfield Publishing, 1997), 151.

If note number 3 were to that same source, just a different page, the entry would read

      3. Ibid., 159.

CMS Style for Citing Electronic Sources

The CMS style for citing electronic sources is still evolving. The pattern for unchangeable sources presented here comes from the current (14th) edition. The pattern for changeable sources comes from the adaptation of CMS style by Kate Turabian (cited on the previous page). An excellent online source for more information about adapting CMS style for online documents is the CMS FAQ available at <http://www. press.uchicago.edu/ Misc/Chicago/cmosfaq.html>.

CD-ROMS and Other Portable Databases

For unchangeable electronic sources, the citation is like that for print sources, with the addition of the name of the producer or vendor and any access numbers associated with the document. Here is a sample entry:

      1. Frank Morring, Jr., "Russian Hardware Allows Earlier Station Experiments," <u>Aviation Week & Space Technology,</u> 16 May 1994, 57; Abstract 15482317: InfoTrac General Periodicals Index-A [CD-ROM], September 1996.

Online Sources

For changeable sources, the entry contains the usual elements for print sources, followed by an indication in square brackets of what type of document it is, the complete document address, and the date of access.

      2. Charles Shepherdson, "History and the Real: Foucault with Lacan," <u>Postmodern Culture</u> 5, no. 2 (January 1995) [serial online]; available from http://jefferson.village.virginia.edu/pmc/ shepherd.195.html; Internet; accessed 15 May 1995.

QUICK VIEW
MODERN LANGUAGE ASSOCIATION (MLA) AUTHOR-PAGE STYLE

MLA style uses parenthetical citations within the text. They lead readers to a list of entries at the end of the document called *Works Cited*. Generally, the material within the parenthetical citation includes the author's name and the page number to which you are referring. Here we summarize briefly the MLA style of documentation, and on the next page we go into more detail about the MLA style for citing electronic sources. If you want more details about MLA documentation style, consult the *MLA Handbook for Writers of Research Papers*, 5th edition (1999). A basic MLA citation in the text will look like this:

　...leads to better research (Morring 57).

This citation would lead readers to the following entry at the end of the document:

　Morring, Frank, Jr. "Russian Hardware Allows
　Earlier Space Station Experiments." <u>Aviation Week
　and Space Technology</u> 16 (May 1994): 57.

Citations in the Text
In MLA style, parenthetical citations go at the end of the sentence in which the source material appears. If the sentence already includes the author's name, then only the page number appears in the parenthetical citation. In the case of more than one work by the same author, a short title is added in the parentheses. The page number is given in the parentheses, without *p.* or *pp.*

Parenthetical citations for direct quotations in the text appear after the closing quotation mark but before the final punctuation. Direct quotations that are more than four lines long should be indented an inch rather than enclosed in quotation marks. The parenthetical reference for such quotations follows the quotation's final punctuation.

Entries in the Works Cited List
The list of works cited includes only sources mentioned in the text and not all sources consulted. Entries are arranged alphabetically by the author's last name (or by the first significant word in the title if there is no author). The page is double spaced, with the first line of each entry flush left and subsequent lines indented half an inch (or five spaces on a typewriter). The basic pattern of an entry is author's name, title, and publication information (place, name of publisher, date, and page numbers).

MLA Style for Citing Electronic Sources

The MLA style for citing electronic sources is still evolving. Presented here is information from the current *MLA Handbook* (1999) as supplemented by MLA's Web site <http://www.mla.org/style/sources.htm>.

CD-ROMs and Other Portable Databases

For unchangeable sources, the citation in the *Works Cited* list includes the author, title, and date information just as for print documents. After the title of the database, there is a period, followed by the producer's name and date of the product, if available. Finally, include the date you accessed the information.

> Morring, Frank, Jr. "Russian Hardware Allows
> Earlier Space Station Experiments." <u>Aviation Week</u>
> <u>and Space Technology</u> 16 (May 1994): 57. <u>InfoTrac:</u>
> <u>General Periodicals Index</u>. 10 Oct. 1998.

Online Sources

For changeable sources, use this format: author's name, full title (articles in quotation marks, books underlined) and any larger document of which it is a part, date of publication or most recent revision, date accessed, and the full URL address enclosed in angle brackets (< >). Here are two examples:

> Shepherdson, Charles. "History and the Real:
> Foucault with Lacan." <u>Postmodern Culture</u> 5.2 (Jan.
> 1995). 15 May 1995
> <http://jefferson.village.virginia.
> edu/pmc/shepherd.195.html>.

> Harnack, Andrew, and Gene Kleppinger. "Beyond the
> MLA Handbook: Documenting Electronic Sources on
> the Internet." <u>Kairos</u> 1.2 (1996). 10 Oct. 1996
> <http://english.ttu.edu/kairos/1.2>.

Ideally, the URL should not be interrupted by a line break; however, if it is too long to fit on one line, break the URL after a period or slash. The same form is used for a document retrieved from a file transfer protocol (FTP) archive, except the abbreviation ftp precedes the address, and the URL is not enclosed in angle brackets.

CHAPTER THREE
COMMUNICATING ON THE INTERNET

Chapter One of this guide explained some of the most important ways people use the Internet to find information. The subject of this chapter is how to use the Internet to communicate with other people. Of course, making a distinction between these two activities is misleading. For example, when you join an e-mail listserv on the subject of technical communication <listserv@listserv.okstate.edu> because you want to learn more about the field and maybe find an internship, your primary motive may be communication, but you are certainly also finding information.

Communicating on the Internet takes many forms. Here is an overview of the topics discussed in this section:

- E-mail—How to send e-mail to your friends all over the world, how to read e-mail addresses, and how to use Internet mail.

- Netiquette—What you should and shouldn't do when you are communicating on the Internet.

- Discussion groups—How to subscribe to listserv mailing lists (and how to unsubscribe), how to take part in Usenet newsgroups.

- Real-time communication—What is Internet Relay Chat (IRC); what are MOOs, MUDs, MUSHs, and WOOs; what is videoconferencing?

- Electronic file transfer—An introduction to File Transfer Protocol (FTP) and how to do it.

- Risks and precautions—Find out what you need to know about computer security, disclosing personal information, copyright, libel, plagiarism, and viruses.

How to Communicate with E-Mail

E-mail is a way of sending messages electronically. If you get e-mail service through an ISP, you will be given a mailbox and software for reading and storing your mail, for composing and sending messages, and for creating mailing lists. There are lots of different e-mail software packages available, but they all work in much the same way. Most Web browsers such as Netscape and Explorer have built-in e-mail software.

When someone sends you a message, it will be temporarily stored on your ISP's mail server. You will use your e-mail software to see if you have any messages waiting. If you do, the e-mail software will download them from the mail server to your computer, where you can read, store, delete, reply to, print, or forward them.

When you get an e-mail account, you will be given an e-mail address. The address has three parts: for example, user_name@domain_name. Usually, you will be able to create your own user name, which is how your mailbox is identified. The "at" sign (@) separates the user name from the domain name. The domain name is the name of the computer or system where your e-mail is stored.

In the above e-mail address, "user_name" and "domain_name" have no spaces (which is indicated by the underscore)—e-mail addresses cannot have any spaces. The address is also in all lowercase, because e-mail addresses are not case sensitive and are easier to read and type without caps. If you get mail returned because the address could not be found, make sure you have entered it correctly. If you have, and the mail is still returned, the person may have changed addresses or may be having problems with the mail system.

Internet Mail

Internet mail (e-mail sent over the Internet) takes e-mail a step further. For example, suppose you are surfing the Web and find a page that has great information, and you want to get in touch with the person who created the page. Usually, the person who created the page will include a link for sending e-mail. When you click the link, a window will appear where you can type and send a message. However, you need **SMTP (simple mail transfer protocol)** to send the message. Check with your ISP for the name of its SMTP server. To receive Internet e-mail, you will also need a **POP (post office protocol)** server. Check with your ISP for a list of services to see if POP mail accounts are available.

Virtual Communities: Listservs and Newsgroups

Virtual communities are ways of organizing or connecting people of like interests over the Internet. The following section discusses some modes of communication that are analogous to print newsletters.

Listserv Mailing Lists

Listservs are servers that house **mailing lists.** Listserv mailing lists are discussion groups categorized by special interest. Unlike Usenet newsgroups, which let you browse messages posted on Usenet (discussed next), listserv mail messages are sent directly to your e-mail address. When a member posts a message to the listserv, the message is delivered to every subscriber.

When you subscribe, your name and e-mail address are added to the mailing list. From that point on, you will receive all e-mail messages that

Info Byte: Netiquette

As with all human communities, even virtual ones, there is acceptable and unacceptable behavior. **Netiquette,** the guidelines for communicating with others on the Internet, helps us all respect the people who share our cyberspace. Most netiquette guidelines are just common sense, a reminder that even though we're in cyberspace, our relations with others are still human relations. Here are some tips:

- Do not use foul or abusive language.

- Do not force offensive material on unwilling participants.

- Do not join in **flaming** (by sending cruel e-mail to someone). Usually, flaming is started over not-so-commonsense breaches of netiquette.

- Do not shout (that is, do not use all caps) at other people on the Internet.

- Do not take off on tangents that are too far from a discussion group's stated purpose.

- Do not post ambiguous questions or ask questions that are answered in a group's Frequently Asked Questions (FAQ) list.

- Be careful to avoid **spamming,** or sending the same message (like a sales pitch) to many different addresses, especially listservs. Spamming is the equivalent of junk mail and will get you flamed in no time.

- Reread your Internet messages before sending them. Something written in haste may be misread.

- Lurk before you leap. (People who subscribe to a listserv and read its messages but do not post any of their own are said to be lurking.) Lurk for a couple of weeks and give yourself a chance to learn that virtual community's rules and temperament before you start posting. This precaution can protect you from making **newbie** mistakes and possibly getting flamed as a result.

are posted to the group. It is always wise to **lurk** (hang out and just read messages) for a while before joining the discussion. When you reply to an e-mail message from a listserv, you can mail the person who sent the message originally or you can post your response to the entire group.

One way to find a listserv for people with a particular interest is to do a key word search on a search engine, such as Yahoo! or AltaVista, by entering the topic and the word `listserv`. Or you can use the extensive mailing lists categorized by subject at "Liszt, the Mailing List Directory" <http://www.liszt.com>.

To subscribe to a list, send an e-mail message to the listserv address. Do not put anything in the subject line of the message. Then, on the first line of the body of the message, type the following:

SUB listname your full name

Once you subscribe, you will receive a set of instructions for list members. It will tell you where to post messages (usually a different address than the subscription address) and what subscription options you have (such as "digest," which combines each day's postings into one packet, or "unsubscribe"). Be sure to save this message!

To unsubscribe, send an e-mail message to the listserv subscription address. Again, do not put anything in the subject line of the message. Then, on the first line of the body of the message, type the following:

UNSUB listname your full name

Remember to unsubscribe if you terminate your e-mail account. Only you can unsubscribe your name from a list.

Usenet Newsgroups

Usenet is a computer network accessible on the Internet that is mainly used for discussion groups. **Newsgroups** are discussion groups on Usenet organized by interest categories. Newsgroups are essentially sets of archived messages, articles, or postings. You are free to browse any newsgroup's articles.

To access newsgroups, you need a newsreader. Most graphic browsers, such as Netscape and Explorer, come equipped with a newsreader. The next thing you need to know is the Network News Transfer Protocol (NNTP) server. Contact your ISP to find out the name of its NNTP server. Once you find out your NNTP server, you will need to adjust your Preferences setup. You will usually be given the choice to edit Mail and News Preferences, and you will find a space to add the name of the NNTP server. When you have finished, save your changes. You may have to restart your browser for the change to take effect. Now you can use the browser's newsreader to browse and respond to newsgroup discussions.

Newsgroups have many **threads** of discussion. A thread is the original message that begins a discussion and all of the replies to that message. Most browsers have options for following threads. For example, when you pull up a newsgroup article in Netscape, there are links at the top of the article to all of the messages in that thread.

Newsgroup articles can literally be here today and gone tomorrow. Because of the thousands of articles a newsgroup can receive in a day, old articles are deleted to make room for the new ones. Depending on how busy a newsgroup is, articles may be deleted within several hours. If you find an article you may want to refer to later, save or print a copy, because it may not be there the next time you look. To save a document as a file on your computer's hard drive, select Save from the File menu and choose a destination.

When accessing newsgroups, some of your basic options are to browse, read, or save newsgroup messages; to reply only to the person who posted a message or to the entire newsgroup; or to post a new message that starts a thread of discussion. Most newsreaders will have buttons for each of these options. As with listservs, it is a good idea to lurk on a newsgroup before you become an active member. To get an idea of what kinds of topics are appropriate, find out if the newsgroup has a **FAQ (frequently asked questions)** page. Newsgroup members will become irate if you post questions that are already discussed in the FAQ, and they will not appreciate messages that discuss topics beyond the scope of their newsgroup. If you make either of these mistakes, you could get flamed—bombarded with irate mail messages! (See Info Byte: Netiquette, page 32.)

Virtual Communities: Real-Time Communication

Real-time communication is different from the various forms of delayed communication that we have discussed so far—e-mail, listservs, and newsgroups. In real time, your messages—whether text, audio, or video—are seen almost instantaneously by those on your channel, instead of being sent and read later by the recipient. There are two main methods of real-time communication—chat groups via **IRC (Internet Relay Chat)** and multiuser domains (MUDs, MOOs, MUSHs, etc.).

To participate in real-time communication, you need some special software. Chat groups, MUDs, MOOs, and videoconferences each require different software; sometimes, different software is even required from chat room to chat room, from MUD to MUD, and so on. This section provides an overview of some of the real-time communication options, as well as links to some Web sites to help you get started. And remember, the same netiquette (see page 32) for other forms of communication is still in effect in real time. For example, avoid shouting (addressing people in all caps), and be careful not to divulge too much personal information.

Internet Relay Chat
Internet Relay Chat (IRC) is a protocol that gives you the ability to communicate in real time with people worldwide through **chat** groups. Once you have the proper software in place, you can connect to an IRC server. After

you are connected to the server, you can sign on to one of the channels and communicate with others who are signed on to the same channel. You can have public conversation, where everyone on the channel is included, or a private conversation between you and one other person. Remember, though, that in IRC channels, the channel moderator can kick you off and refuse you future access, so follow netiquette (see page 32).

A good place to begin is with a document called The IRC Prelude, available at <http://www.irchelp.org/irchelp/>. Useful software that you can download is mIRC (a graphic client) at the address above, or LisztIRC at <www.liszt.com/chat/intro.html>. This page also provides IRC FAQs.

MUDs, MOOs, MUSHs, and WOOs

The first multiuser programming option was the **MUD (Multiuser Domain [Dimension, or Dungeon])**. A MUD is a computer program that creates a world for users to log on to (usually by Telnet). Users can participate in role playing, assuming various characters or personae. The next to come along were the **MOO (MUD Object-Oriented environment)** and the **MUSH (Multiuser Shared Hallucination)**. MOOs, MUSHs, and other multiuser domains are similar. They all have a gathering of users, usually role playing, but MOOs and MUSHs allow for physical objects to be placed in the virtual room where the participants are gathered. Among the latest in multiuser technology is the **WOO (Web Object-Oriented environment)**, where Web hypermedia capabilities are combined with MOO technology. These forms of real-time communication started out as ways to facilitate multiuser games. Now they are being used to create virtual societies. For beginner information, see the Megabyte University's Discussion List page at <http://www.daedalus.com/MBU/MBU.intro.html>. For more advanced information, see <www.csl.sony.co.jp/project/VS/index.html>.

A good place to get started with multiuser options is the Pueblo site at <http://www.chaco.com/pueblo/contents.html>. Pueblo is an example of client software needed to participate in virtual communities; this site also provides some general information and FAQs on multiuser communities.

Videoconferencing

Videoconferencing allows you and other people around the world who are signed on to the same conference, and who have the required audio and video software and hardware, to see and hear each other. You can also show each other images and text. One of the most popular software packages for videoconferencing is CU-SeeMe. For more information on videoconferencing, including CU-SeeMe and other software, go to <http://rocketcharged.com/cu-seeme/>.

File Transfer Protocol (FTP)

FTP (file transfer protocol) allows you to send or retrieve files from one computer to another. In reference to the Internet, it usually means downloading files (such as text files and software programs) from the Internet to your computer. You can download huge amounts of software for free or for a minimal charge at FTP archives, such as Shareware.com at <http://www. shareware.com>.

To download a file from an FTP archive, you need to log in with a user name and password. Most FTP archives use anonymous FTP, meaning that you use the word "anonymous" as your user name and your e-mail address as your password. Browsers equipped with FTP software will do this automatically, so that when you click on a file you want to download, it will begin downloading immediately.

The Internet provides a vast number of downloadable files, such as HTML editors (used for creating Web pages), chat software, graphics animators, games (including virtual reality), and screen savers. The easiest way to find these files is to go directly to a file archive, such as Shareware.com, where you can do a key word search, search the New Arrivals, or browse Most Popular Selections (the most often downloaded selections). Much of the software is free, called **freeware.** Some software, called **shareware,** requires a small fee. (Don't let Shareware.com's name fool you; most of its software is free.) In addition to Shareware.com, a good place to find software (as well as reviews and ratings of software) is ZDNet at <http://www.zdnet.com>.

You can search for other FTP archives by using the search engine Archie, but Archie is not as user friendly as most of the search engines discussed so far. With Archie, you need to know the name of the software for which you are looking. There is also a Web-based interface for using Archie, called ArchiePlex. You can find a list of ArchiePlex servers at <http://cuiwww.unige.ch/archie.html>. Even though ArchiePlex is Web-based, it is still rather difficult to use, so read the instructions carefully before beginning any searches.

Most graphic Web browsers, such as Netscape and Explorer, come equipped with FTP software. However, this software is usually restricted to downloading files and is not capable of sending files. In order to send files, you need full-service FTP software, which you can download for free. For the Macintosh, you can get Fetch at <http://www.dartmouth.edu/pages/softdev/fetch.html>, or, for a PC, you can get a free limited version of WS_FTP at <http://www.ipswitch.com/cgi/download_eval.pl?product=main>.

Risks and Precautions

The following section deals with some of the risks that you may encounter while working with the Internet. We also suggest some precautions that may help you avoid the most common pitfalls.

Privacy

It is not a good idea to put anything in an e-mail message that you would not want others to see, because messages can be intercepted or sent to the wrong person. Especially if the computer you are using (or your receiver is using) belongs to your school or employer, your messages are very easy for others to access. There are privacy programs available, but using such a program may make people suspect that something secret is going on.

If you turn your computer into a server, you can have problems with individuals being able to access documents and information on your machine other than what you want to publish.

Personal Security

Sometimes you may be asked to give personal information on the Internet, especially when downloading commercial software. Reputable businesses have taken precautions to ensure the security of the information you provide. However, if you are unsure of the vendor (or whenever you sign on to online news services), you should make a rule of giving just your first or last name and not giving your home address or phone number.

If you publish your own Web page (discussed in Chapter Four), be aware that your page is accessible to the public. You want to give careful consideration to the amount and kind of personal information that you post on your page, such as your picture, phone numbers, and addresses. It is one thing for the whole world to have your e-mail address; it may be quite another for the whole world to be able to recognize you on sight and drive to where you live.

Copyright

It is safe to assume that most of the material on the Internet is copyrighted. *The absence of a copyright notice does not mean that the material is not protected* or that it can be assumed to be in the public domain and therefore usable without seeking permission from the author or copyright holder. (For posting on the Web, however, the recommended procedure is to put "Copyright," the copyright symbol [©], the date published, the owner's name, and "All rights reserved" on documents that fall under copyright protection.) The only exception to using material from print sources that is protected by a copyright is "fair use," which usually means reproduction of a limited amount of material for educational purposes, criticism, comment, or news reporting. For more information on copyright issues, see <http://lcweb.loc.gov/copyright>.

Ideas, facts, titles, names, short phrases, and blank forms are not protected by copyright. Items in the public domain, such as government documents or items for which copyright has expired, are not protected by copyright and may be used without permission.

Libel

When someone knowingly spreads false information about another person, harming that person's reputation, or defaming them, it is called slander. However, when such information is published in print, it is defamatory writing and may be considered libelous. The same caution applies to writing published on the Web, so make sure that any information you post is true and verifiable. Libel is a crime and is punishable as a felony.

Plagiarism

For Web documents, you can create a link to someone's Web page, but *you may not* cut and paste any part of someone's Web page and place it on your own. Similarly, if you quote Web-page information in a written document, you must cite it properly. (See the section on documentation, starting on page 19.)

Viruses

Viruses can be devastating to your computer. They can damage or destroy both hardware and software. Viruses can get into your computer in several ways. One way is to put an infected disk into your computer's disk drive and open a file on it. Viruses can also be downloaded from the Internet when you transfer files to your computer—for example, by downloading software or text files. Viruses can also be sent via e-mail: Reading a message is not generally a problem, but if you open an attachment contaminated with a virus, your computer will become infected. Basically, if you do anything with e-mail beyond reading the message itself, your computer is susceptible to viruses.

You can use virus protection software to detect viruses and even prevent them from contaminating your computer. Some computers come with anti-virus software, but you can also purchase software or download it from the Internet. For the latest on computer viruses and anti-virus software, visit IBM's "Antivirus Online" at <http://www.av.ibm.com/current/FrontPage/>, the Federal Computer Incident Response Capability (FedCirc) site at <http://www.fedcirc.gov>, or the Department of Energy's Incident Advisory Capability site at <http://ciac.llnl.gov/>. At these sites, you will find information such as virus names, reviews of anti-virus software, and which viruses are currently at large.

Time Management

You can waste twenty-four hours a day, seven days a week, on the Internet if you are not careful. A good practice, therefore, is to separate "fun" Web sessions from "work" Web sessions. Determine before you begin a Web session which kind of session you intend it to be and how much time you can give to it. Then stick to your plans.

CHAPTER FOUR
FINDING INTERNSHIPS AND JOBS
ON THE INTERNET

When you start looking for internships or jobs, the Internet has searchable databases of job postings by employers worldwide. This use of the Internet is one of its fastest-growing areas and one that is especially important for students. Depending on the position you are looking for, you can search by type of job, key word, or your skills, and by city, state, or country.

Sites to Search for Jobs

With services like The Career Search Launch Pad at <http://www.pantos. org/cslp>, you can access several job-search engines. The Web pages available from the Launch Pad are Career Mosaic, NationJob, Online Career Center, and Net Temps. You can access these career-search engines directly from the Launch Pad Web page, or you can link directly to each of them, using the URLs given below. These are just a few of our favorite sites; you can find more on Mayfield's Web page at <http://www.mayfieldpub.com/ EnglishDepartment/resources/jobsinterns.htm>.

America's Job Bank <http://www.ajb.dni.us/>

Career Mosaic <http://www.careermosaic.com>

Monster.Com <http://www.monster.com>

NationJob <http://www.nationjob.com>

Online Career Center <http://www.occ.com>

Net Temps <http://www.net-temps.com>

 Info Bit—Many of the job-finding services allow you to post your own résumé in their databank, which can make it easier for employers who are looking for someone with your unique blend of education and experiences. Usually, to post your résumé you will need to have a version written in HTML. The section on creating your own Web page (pages 41–43) will get you off to a good start in creating an HTML version of your résumé.

Internships
A great place to start looking for internships is Yahoo!'s Internships category at <http://dir.yahoo.com/Education/Career_and_Vocational/

Career_Planning/Internships/>. Some other listings are:

- Intern-Net
  http://www.InternshipPrograms.com/
- JobTrak
  http://www.jobtrak.com/
- JobWeb
  http://www.jobweb.org
- Princeton Review
  http://www.review.com/career/find/intern.cfm

You can also find internships listed on the Web under particular fields (such as journalism), or particular locations (such as Washington, D.C.), or with particular companies (simply find your target employer's Web page and search it for an internships section).

Scholarships

To find scholarship opportunities, go to Yahoo!'s scholarship site at <http://search.yahoo.com/search?p=scholarships>. Another good list may be found at <http://sandburg.unm.edu/>.

Creating Your Own Web Pages

To post your own Web pages, you first need to make sure that your ISP has the ability to house them. There is usually an extra fee to store Web pages, so check to see what the rates are. Once you have a place to store your pages, the next step is to learn HTML. HTML uses **tags** contained in angle brackets, < >, to mark up the text of your document. Basically, HTML tags act as a set of instructions for the Web browser (such as Netscape); the tags tell the browser how your Web page should look (what's bold, what's in color, where pictures go) and how to respond to mouse clicks and keyboard strokes (if someone clicks on a link, where the browser should take them, or what Web page or file you are linking to). If you are not familiar with HTML, there is an excellent tutorial (created by Eric Meyer for Case Western University) called "Introduction to HTML" at <http://www.cwru.edu/help/introHTML/>. Also, after you start working with HTML, it's a good idea to have a cheat sheet with all the HTML tags. For such a list, go to the Bare Bones Guide for HTML 4.0 (or the most current version) by Kevin Werbach at <http://werbach.com/barebones/>.

Guidelines for Web-page design. In many ways, good Web-page design follows the same principles as good page design in general—the document should be professional in appearance, important design elements should be used in a consistent way, and the document should be easy for readers to use (you can find more on how these principles apply to print pages in *Easy Access,* Second Edition, by Michael Keene and Katherine Adams, Mayfield, 1999). Here's how these principles apply to Web pages:

- **The document should be professional in appearance.** Chiefly, this means the page should not be cluttered. Think of your screen as being divided into, at most, three blocks, with each block holding a different kind of element (text, links, visuals). Keeping background ("wallpaper") material to a minimum also helps keep the page uncluttered. The major sections of the document itself should be indicated by headings, lists should be separated from text, and any data should be displayed in simple tables. Adding a link to your e-mail address and a "last updated" date are good finishing touches for giving your page a professional appearance.

- **Important design elements should be used in a consistent way.** "White space"—areas of the page in which nothing is printed—is critical to the design of print publications, and at least equally critical to Web-page design. The temptation for a newbie is to fill every pixel with colors and patterns. The logic, apparently, is, if there's any open space left at all, it's better to fill it with yet another dancing baby. But white space doesn't lie, and using lots of it in your Web page will really help the page's design. Use white space around the edges, at the tops and bottoms of screens, and especially between elements, whether vertical or horizontal. Instead of making long, endless pages, break text and graphics into shorter, linked pages. Try to stick with just one or two typefaces throughout, rather than seeing how many different ones you can use.

- **The document should be easy for readers to use.** Keep each Web page short, and keep your pages up-to-date. Especially on the "front" pages, try to shorten loading time by limiting visuals at least a little bit. When you do use images, try to keep the files small.

If you keep your Web pages uncluttered, use lots of white space, and make sure your pages load quickly, you're on your way to producing well-designed pages. Check your page on different machines and on different browsers to make sure that it looks the way you want it to. Also, remember that the information you are posting is available to anyone, so be careful what kind of personal information you post, such as pictures, phone numbers, and addresses (see "Personal Security," page 37).

Once you have your Web pages ready for the rest of the world, the final step is to make them available through search engines (such as Yahoo! or AltaVista). For other people to be able to look up your page with a search engine, you have to submit it. Of course it would be quite time consuming to submit your page to each search engine. To help make this task easier, sign up for a free trial account from Submit It! at <http://www.submitit. com>. Have fun!

Sending Your Résumé Electronically

If you have your résumé on the Web in HTML, prospective employers can view it and download it or print it out as needed. If you do not have your résumé in that form, you may be asked to e-mail it to a prospective employer. In that case, here are a few pointers to remember: E-mail programs today do not handle things like different type fonts or sizes, boldface type, or italics; and fancy spacing (centering, lists that use hanging indents, etc.) usually just contributes to a document that comes out on the other end in a mess. If there is a chance you will need to e-mail your résumé, you need a very plain version—one in which all headings are at the left margin, only one typeface is used (you can do some differentiation with uppercase letters, use asterisks instead of bullets, etc.), and, in general, all that fancy typography that makes your print or HTML résumé look so snazzy is gone. If you use a plain version, then your prospective employer just might get your résumé in an ungarbled form.

Putting your résumé into an attachment to a piece of e-mail is not a good idea, because there's no guarantee at all that the person receiving that attachment has a program to open it that will be compatible with the program you used to create it. You're better off just to paste your résumé right into the body of your e-mail. Finally, remember that once you e-mail your résumé to someone, chances are that person is going to enter it into an electronic database that holds thousands of résumés, so that individuals within the company looking for new hires with particular qualifications can let their computers search the database for the key words that name those skills. What key words can be found on your résumé, and are they the right ones?

CHAPTER FIVE
INTERNET RESOURCES

Reference Material

Dictionaries and Thesauruses
- Bartlett's Quotations (1901 ed.)
  http://www.bartleby.com/99
- Merriam Webster's Dictionary and Thesaurus
  http://www.m-w.com/home.htm
- Roget's Thesaurus (version 1.02)
  http://www.thesaurus.com
- Strunk's Elements of Style (1918 ed.)
  http://www.bartleby.com/141

Citations and Copyright
You can start with the copyright office at the Library of Congress <http://lcweb.loc.gov/copyright>, and then check "the copyright Web site" at <http://www.benedict.com>. There's a good discussion of citing sources at <http://libweb.sdsu.edu/cite.html>.

Libraries
- Internet Public Library
  http://ipl.org
- Library of Congress
  http://lcweb.loc.gov/library/

Newspapers
Nearly every large-city newspaper has some kind of Web presence now. Some are only small bits of the print newspapers, and others require either registration, or subscription for money, or both, for you to access them. Besides the lists available on Yahoo!, there's a good geographic listing at <http://www.newsrack.com>.

Broadcast News
- CNN
  http://www.cnn.com

- National Public Radio
  http://www.npr.org
- PBS
  http://www.pbs.org

News Filters
Try the combination of **news filter** and screen saver at <http://www.
pointcast.com>

Book Reviews
- BookWire
  http://www.bookwire.com
- The Independent Reader
  http://www.independentreader.com

Online Writing Centers
There's a comprehensive list of these wonderful facilities at the National
Writing Centers Association's home page <http://departments.colgate.edu/
diw/NWCA.html>.

People Finders
Most of the major search engines have people finders (as well as Postal
Service address finders, e-mail address finders, and phone number finders)
available from their home page. For example, you can find Yahoo!'s people
finder at <http://people.yahoo.com>.

Image Finders
It is becoming easier and easier to find particular images (pictures,
paintings, images of any kind) on the Web, with the help of such pages
as Mister Pix <http://www.mister-pix.com>, the AltaVista Photo Finder
<http://www.altavista.com>, and the Yahoo! Image Surfer <http://ipix.
yahoo.com>. If there is an image on the Web that you want to incorporate
in a project, you can copy that image and save it to your computer. Once
it is saved, you can put it on your Web page, put it in a word processing
document, and the like. According to fair-use guidelines, a limited amount
of copyrighted material may be used without permission for educational
purposes, criticism, comment, or news reporting.
    Here's how to grab images from the Web. To save an image, place your
mouse over the image. If you are using a PC, hold down a right-click. If
you are using a Macintosh, hold down a regular click. You will be given a
pop-up menu. From the menu, choose "Save Image As." You will be given

a box with options for a file name (be sure to keep the same extension if you change the file name, e.g., **.gif** or **.jpg**) and a file location (to put it in the folder and drive of your choice). Once the file is saved, you can open the image in a graphics program, such as Adobe Photoshop or Super Paint. You can choose to "Copy" it. You can then place the image in a word processing document. Once it is copied, open your word processor to the file where you want the image placed, and "Paste" it. If you want to place the image in a Web page, then save the image to the appropriate folder, and reference the file in the HTML file.

Remember: You should assume that just about everything on the Web is protected by copyright. Material does not have to have a copyright symbol on it to be so protected. Fair-use guidelines may be followed for use of copyrighted material without permission in student papers and projects.

CHAPTER SIX
PSYCHOLOGY AND THE INTERNET

In addition to the printed resources available in your library, the Internet offers you many new options for research. From the spark of insight that begins a research project through the publishing guidelines for your final paper, the Internet can be a valuable ally at every step of the research process. These steps can be summarized as:

1. Developing a research idea into a testable hypothesis
2. Choosing a research design (experimental, correlational and so on)
3. Obtaining participants for a study
4. Conducting the study
5. Analyzing the data (using descriptive and inferential statistics)
6. Reporting the results (as a paper or an oral presentation)

Although no printed guide can possibly encompass the millions of pages of information on the Internet, you can use the sites described here as a starting point. As you move through the research process, you can consult this guide at any time.

The most valuable tool in negotiating the Internet is practice, so enter a term into a search engine and explore the resulting list of links as your interest directs you. Above all, enjoy the diversity and freedom of the Internet to explore psychology and to learn at the unprecedented speed of the "information superhighway".

Developing Ideas and Choosing a Design

Search Engines

World Wide Web search engines, as described in Chapter One of this guide, are some of the most valuable tools for finding out what is available on the Internet in the area that you are considering for your research project. Some of the best search engines are:

- Alta Vista
  http://www.altavista.digital.com
- Dog Pile
  http://www.dogpile.com
- Excite
  http://www.excite.com
- Infoseek
  http://infoseek.go.com
- Web Crawler
  http://www.webcrawler.com
- Yahoo!
  http://www.yahoo.com

Alta Vista and Yahoo! are described in more detail in Chapter One. Metacrawler **http:www.metacrawler.com** is a service that explores several search engines at once, providing more comprehensive results, although at a slower rate.

All of these search engines provide methods of complex searching, in which one can look for phrases and include Boolean operators, such as AND, OR, NOT or NEAR. They also allow for searches of both the World Wide Web and Usenet. Given the enormous number of documents available, it is best to search for words and phrases that will be specifically relevant to what you are seeking. For example, if you are looking for information on a specific discipline in psychology, the use of technical words or phrases such as "classical conditioning" or "systematic desensitization" will help make the search engine's response more manageable. AltaVista has features that allow the user to include or exclude a variety of potential key words, helping to narrow a search considerably.

The search engine used to find many of the sites listed in this guide was **http://www.yahoo.com**. Figure 1 displays the home page for the Yahoo! search engine site, current at this time of press. Note that one of the categories you can choose is "Social Science". Following this link will take you to more specific categories, including "Psychology". Figure 2 shows the top of the Psychology category on Yahoo!, current at the time of press. The alphabetical list of sites can link you to many interesting resources on the Internet. Keep in mind that the content is always changing and that some sources are more scientific and reliable than others. You may choose to follow links to even more specific categories until you reach a list of sites that reflect your research goals. Although following links is convenient, it is not necessary. You may enter key words into the Search box at any time.

World Wide Web Resources

The Web is probably the easiest resource for a beginning user of the Internet to grasp. Information is available on almost every conceivable

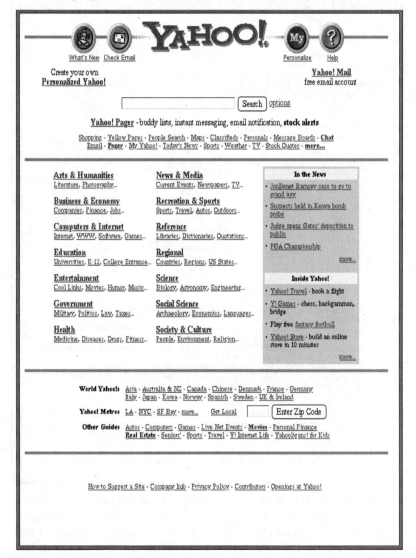

Figure 1   *Home page for the Yahoo! search engine. Text and artwork copyright © 1998 Yahoo! All rights reserved. YAHOO! and the YAHOO! logo are trademarks of YAHOO! Inc.*

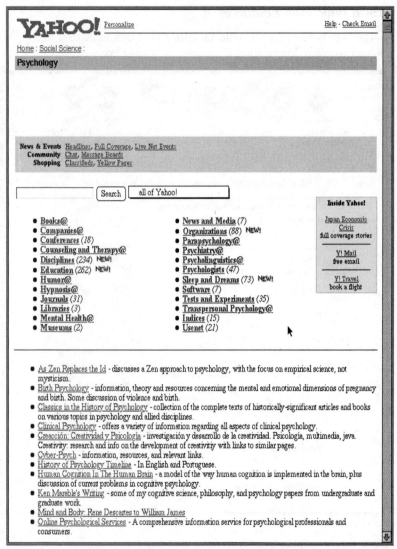

Figure 2 *Clicking on the main category "Social Science" on the Yahoo! home page will give you another set of choices. Clicking on the selection "Psychology" will give you a list of alphabetical categories (shown in bold type) and a list of Web sites similar to the list shown. Using a hierarchial index of topics, or subject tree, is a good method for getting an overview of broadly related pages, whereas the key word method allows you to narrow your search considerably.*

topic. With any of the aforementioned search engines, the term *psychology* will yield thousands of Web sites. It is important to limit your searches to a manageable number, using qualifying terms. A search of the Web using about half a dozen key words relevant to your topic or general idea will yield a significant number of references—depending, of course, on the key words you use.

The following list of psychology Web sites is a good place to start to search for information on all the major topics in this field.

General Resources for Psychology

Organizations

There are many professional organizations in the field of psychology. This section provides a comprehensive list of psychological and psychology-related organizations on the Internet.

- American Psychiatric Association
  The APA is a widely recognized organization that deals with diagnosis and treatment of mental disorders.
  http://www.psych.org
- American Psychology Association
  The APA homepage provides links to all areas of psychology.
  http://www.apa.org/
- American Psychological Society
  This is the professional organization for psychologists.
  http://krantzj.hanover.edu/APS/
- British Psychological Society
  Professional organization for British psychologists.
  http://www.bps.org.uk
- Cognitive Neuroscience Society
  For the latest information of cognitive neuroscience.
  http://www.dartmouth.edu/~cns/
- International Psychoanalytical Association
  The professional organization for psychoanalytic psychology.
  http://www.ipa.org.uk/
- International Society of Political Psychology
  Learn how politics and psychology are interrelated.
  http://ispp.org:80/

- Psi Chi
  Honors organization for psychologists.
  http://www.psichi.org/intro.asp
- Psychology Organizations on the Web
  Provides links to many different psychology related organizations.
  http://www.wesleyan.edu/spn/psych.htm
- Society for Computers in Psychology
  The organization that integrates computer technology with psychology.
  http://www.lafayette.edu/allanr/scip.html
- Society for the Quantitative Analysis of Behavior
  Organization for Behavioral Researchers.
  http://www.jsu.edu/depart/psychology/sebac/sqab.html
- Society for Judgement and Decision Making
  The professional organization for thinking and judgement.
  http://www.sjdm.org:80/sjdm/
- Society for the Psychological Study of Social Issues
  Views social issues through a psychological screen.
  http://www.spssi.org/
- The Federation of Behavioral, Psychological and Cognitive Sciences
  Organization for psychologists in a wide variety of fields.
  http://www.am.org/federation/

Professional Journals in Psychology

   In addition to searching the literature online, you can now use the
Internet to read selected journal articles right from your computer. Many
psychology-specific journals offer full text articles over the Internet. The
following list includes each journal's Web address and a brief description
of the journal found on its Web site.

- American Psychological Association Journals
  "Web site provides a table of contents for a large number of journals
  sponsored by the American Psychological Association."
  http://www.apa.org/journals/
- American Psychologist
  "Integrative articles that draw upon diverse areas of the field and relate
  them to the whole."
  Online: Journal information. Selected abstracts, table of contents for past
  twelve months.
  http://www.apa.org/journals/amp.html

- The APA Monitor
  "Official newspaper of the American Psychological Association."
  Online: Journal information. Free full text articles from 1995.
  http://www.apa.org/monitor

- Behavioral and Brain Sciences
  "Interdisciplinary journal of 'open peer commentary' and 'target articles'
  in psychology, neuroscience, behavioral biology, cognitive science, and
  more".
  Online: Journal information. Free full text articles.
  http://www.princeton.edu/~harnad/bbs/

- Canadian Journal of Behavioral Science
  "Publishes original contributions in the applied areas of psychology."
  Online: Journal information. Free full text articles from 1995.
  http://www.cpa.ca/cjbsnew

- Contemporary Psychology
  "Contains critical reviews of books, films, tapes, and other media relevant
  to psychology."
  Online: Journal information. Free full text articles and selected reviews.
  http://www.apa.org/journals/cnt.html

- Current Research in Social Psychology
  "A peer-reviewed, electronic journal covering all aspects of social
  psychology."
  Online: Journal information. Free full text articles from 1995.
  http://www.uiowa.edu/~grpproc/crisp/crisp.html

- The Industrial-Organizational Psychologist
  "Official newsletter for the Society for Industrial-Organizational
  Psychology"
  Online: Journal information. Free full text articles from 1995.
  http://www.siop.org/TIP.html

- International Bulletin of Political Psychology
  "An electronic weekly designed to sensitize social scientists, public
  officials, mass media representatives, informed citizenry, and social
  activists to the psychology of politics and the politics of psychology."
  Online: Journal information. Free full text articles from 1996.
  http://www.pr.erau.edu/~security/index.html

- The International Journal of Psycho-Analysis
  "Clinical and theoretical topics from the major schools of psychoanalysis."
  Online: Journal information. Abstracts for papers in current issue only.
  http://www.ijpa.org

- International Journal of Psychopathology, Psychopharmacology and Psychotherapy
  "Devoted to innovations in the understanding of psychopathology and in the psychopharmacologic and psychotherapeutic techniques."
  Online: Journal information. Free full text articles from 1996.
  http://www.psycom.net/ijppp.html

- Journal of Clinical Psychoanalysis
  "A journal about clinical techniques and issues in psychoanalysis."
  Online: Journal information. Free full text in selected articles only.
  http://plaza.interport.net/nypsan/jcp.html

- The Journal of Credibility Assessment and Witness Psychology
  "Original, empirical, review and theoretical work in all areas of the scientific study of credibility assessment and witness psychology."
  http://truth.idbsu.edu/jcaawp/default.html

- Journal of Psychology and the Behavioral Sciences
  "Offers undergraduate and graduate students as well as faculty an opportunity to publish in a recognized academic journal."
  Online: Journal information. Free full text articles in selected areas only.
  http://alpha.fdu.edu/psychweb/JPBS.htm

- Pre and Perinatal Psychology Journal
  "Focusing on in-depth explorations of the psychological dimension of human reproduction and pregnancy, and the development of the unborn child".
  Online: Journal information. Free full text articles.
  http://www.birthpsychology.com/journal/index.html

- PsychNews International
  "Provides detailed information on psychology issues around the world."
  Online: Journal information. Free full text articles from 1996.
  http://www.mhnet.org/pni

- Psycoloquy
  "Articles and peer commentary in all areas of psychology."
  Online: Journal information. Free full text articles from 1990.
  http://www.princeton.edu/~harnad/psyc.html

- Der Zeitgeist: The Student Journal of Psychology
  "An electronic journal devoted to publishing work of psychology undergraduate and graduate students."
  http://www.wwu.edu/~n9140024/

Professional Journals in Other Related Areas of Interest

The following list includes journals in fields related to the area of psychology. For each journal you will find the Web address, a description of the journal and contents of the site.

- Behavioral Healthcare Tomorrow Journal
  "Industry news, strategic information and analysis, and solution-focused case studies for leaders in the field of mental health and substance abuse services."
  Online: Journal information. Free full text articles.
  http://www.centralink.com/journal/
- Connexions: A Web Journal for Cognitive Scientists
  "A forum where graduate researchers in philosophy of mind and cognitive science can exchange ideas."
  Online: Journal articles. Free full text articles from 1996.
  http://www.shef.ac.uk/~phil/connex/index.html
- The Harvard Brain
  "Harvard's undergraduate neuroscience magazine."
  Online: Journal information. Free full text articles from 1994.
  http://hcs.harvard.edu/~husn/BRAIN/index.html
- Journal of Applied Behavior Analysis
  Online: Journal information. Free full text on selected articles.
  http://www.envmed.rochester.edu/wwwrap/behavior/jaba/jabahome.htm
- Journal of Artificial Intelligence Research
  "A refereed journal, covering all areas of artificial intelligence."
  http://www.cs.washington.edu/research/jair/home.html
- Journal of Psychiatry and Neuroscience
  "Publishes original research articles and review papers in clinical psychiatry and neuroscience related to major psychiatric disorders."
  http://cpa.medical.org/cpa/public2/publications/jpnintro.htm
- Journal of Experimental Analysis of Behavior
  Online: Journal information. Free full text on selected articles only.
  http://www.envmed.rochester.edu/wwwrap/behavior/jeab/jeabhome.htm
- Neuroscience-Net
  "A scholarly journal devoted to publishing research in basic and clinical neuroscience."
  Online: Journal information. Free full text articles from 1996.
  http://www.neuroscience.com

- Perception
  "A scholarly journal reporting experimental results and theoretical ideas ranging over the fields of human, animal and machine perception."
  Online: Journal information. Free full text on selected articles only.
  http://www.perceptionweb.com

- Psybernetika
  "An electronic journal by and for students."
  Online: Journal information. Free full text articles from 1995.
  http://www.sfu.ca/~wwwpsyb

- PSYCHE
  "An interdisciplinary journal on the research of consciousness."
  Online: Journal information. Free full text articles from 1993.
  http://psyche.cs.monash.edu.au

- Psychiatric News
  "Newspaper of the American Psychiatric Association."
  Online: Journal information. Free full text articles from 1996.
  http://www.appi.org/pnews/pnhome.html

- Psychiatric Times
  "Provides the latest information in the field of psychiatry."
  Online: Journal information. Free full text articles from 1994.
  http://www.mhsource.com/psychiatrictimes.html

- Psychiatry On-Line
  "Electronic journal of psychiatric news and research."
  Online: Journal information. Free full text articles from 1994.
  http://www.priory.co.uk/psych.htm

General Resources for Research and Analysis: Twenty Key Areas of Psychology

Abnormal and Clinical Psychology

- Alzheimer's Association
  This site is dedicated to the research for the causes, cures and prevention of Alzheimer's disease.
  http://www.alz.org

- Anxiety
  Site contains information about various anxiety disorders, types of support and treatment.
  http://stressrelease.com/checklist.html

- Ask NOAH About–Mental Health
  New York Online Access to Health provides fact sheets and links to all
  types of mental health issues.
  http://www.noah.cuny.edu/illness/mentalhealth/mental.html

- Attention Deficit Disorder
  Information about diagnosing and treating ADD.
  http://www.chadd.org/
  http://www.health-center.com/english/brain/adhd/

- Autism
  Site on the causes, support and treatment for this childhood disorder.
  http://www.autism.org/

- Clinical Psychology Resources
  Connections to specific psychological disorders, clinical assessment and
  psychotherapy.
  http://www.psychologie.uni-bonn.de/kap/links_20.htm

- Depression
  Site provides information about diagnosis and treatments for this
  disorder.
  http://execpc.com/~corbeau/

- Mood Disorders
  General information about diagnosis and treatment of all the affective
  disorders.
  http://www.psych.helsinki.fi/~janne/mood/mood.html

- National Alliance for the Mentally Ill (NAMI)
  Provides information to family and friends of the mentally ill.
  http://www.cais.com/vikings/nami/index.html

- National Attention Deficit Disorder Association (NADDA)
  Devoted to information about ADD and ADHD, including diagnosis and
  treatment.
  http://ww.add.org

- National Institute of Mental Health (NIMH)
  Designed to conduct and support research on mental illness and mental
  health issues.
  http://www.nimh.nih.gov

- National Tourette Syndrome Association (NTSA)
  Site dedicated to diagnosis and treatment of Tourette Syndrome.
  http://neuro-www2.mgh.harvard.edu/tsa/tsamain.nclk

- Online Psych: Mental Health Forum
  Provides detailed information about mental health issues and sources.
  http://www.allhealth.com/onlinepsych/
- The Schizophrenia Home Page
  Information about diagnosis, causes and treatments of schizophrenia.
  http://www.schizophrenia.com/

Artificial Intelligence

- Artificial Intelligence: WWW Virtual Library
  Provides updated information about research on artificial intelligence.
  http://www.cs.reading.ac.uk/people/dwc/ai.html

Biological Issues in Psychology

- Brain Briefings
  Wide variety of articles about the brain and its functioning.
  http://www.sfn.org/briefings/
- Probe the Brain
  An interactive site to explore the human brain.
  http://www.pbs.org/wgbh/aso/tryit/brain/
- The Brain: A Work in Progress
  Articles, information and links to sources about the brain.
  http://www.latimes.com/home/news/science/reports/thebrain/
- The Brain Puzzle
  Site to explore your knowledge about the human brain.
  http://www.dana.org/brainweek/puzzle99.html
- The Endocrine System
  Information and diagrams about the endocrine and hormonal system.
  http://www.healthdirect.com/usechk/endocrin.htm

Cognition and Thinking Processes

- Basics of Cognitive Psychology
  Site explores the basic principles of cognitive psychology.
  http://mindstreet.com/cbt.html
- Cognitive and Psychological Sciences on the Internet
  Explore issues related to cognitive psychology on this site.
  http://matia.stanford.edu/cogsci/

• Cognitive Science Sites on Yahoo!
Variety of sites related to the study of cognitive science.
http://dir.yahoo.com/science/cognitive_science/

Consciousness

• Consciousness
Discussion and research about consciousness and altered states of consciousness.
http://psyche.cs.monash.edu.au/

• Consciousness Research Library
Library provides information about a variety of human consciousness experiences.
http://eeyore.lvhrc.nevada.edu/~cogno/cogno.html

Developmental Psychology (Infant, Child, Adolescent, and Aging)

• Adolescent Psychiatry
AACAP provides information about adolescent psychiatric disorders and treatments.
http://www.aacap.org/web/aacap

• Birth Defects
Extensive information about types, causes and treatments of birth defects.
http://www.birthdefects.org/

• Developmental Biology Embryo Development
Site studies cellular development in embryos.
http://sdb.bio.purdue.edu/other/vl_db.html

• Diving into the Gene Pool
Exploratorium provides interactive discussion on modern genetics.
http://www.exploratorium.edu/genepool/

• Down Syndrome
Information provided about causes of this type of mental retardation.
http://www.ndss.org/

• Genetics
Learn about the Human Genome Project and latest genetic research.
http://www.genenet.com/

- Introduction to Mental Retardation
  Covers definitions and commonly asked questions about mental
  retardation.
  http://TheArc.org/faqs/mrqa.html

- Language Development
  Site discusses work of Noam Chomsky on language development.
  http://www.worldmedia.com/archive

- Mental Health Risk Factors for Adolescents
  Comprehensive guide to adolescent mental health issues.
  http://education.indiana.edu/cas/adol/mental.html

- Institute for Brain Aging and Dementia
  Information provided about causes and treatments for dementia and
  other brain aging diseases.
  http://teri.bio.uci.edu

Ethical Issues and Research in Psychology

- Animal Rights Coalition
  Discusses ethical treatment of animals in research.
  http://www.priment.com/~skyblew/arc/arc.html

- Bad Science
  Site discusses how much research is based on bad science and incorrect
  assumptions.
  http://www.ems.psu.edu/~fraser/BadScience.html

- Ethical Principles of Psychologists and Code of Conduct
  Complete code of ethics and principles that govern psychological
  research.
  http://www.apa.org/ethics/code.html

- Lab Animal
  Explains how animal research is conducted and the guidelines followed.
  http://www.labanimal.com

- Psychological Research on the Net
  Links to psychology-related famous experiments.
  http://psych.hanover.edu/APS/exponnet.html

Health Psychology

• Stress, Anxiety and Fears
Site that gives comprehensive information about sources and treatments for stress and anxiety related disorders.
http://www.cmhc.com/psyhelp/chap5/

History of Psychology

• Classics in the History of Psychology
Information about famous historical events and classic discoveries in psychology.
http://www.yorku.ca/dept/psych/classics
• The History of Psychology
University Brunswick course with related psychology links.
http://www.unb.ca/web/units/psych/likely/psyc4053.htm
• Today in the History of Psychology
Site provides information on important historical events in psychology.
http://www.cwu.edu/~warren/today.html

Human Sexuality

• AIDS Information
Up-to-date information about AIDS and HIV treatments and prevention.
http://www.cdcnac.org/
• Sexual Orientation and Homosexuality
Answers to basic questions about sexual orientation and homosexuality.
http://www.apa.org/pubinfo/orient.html
• Society for Human Sexuality
Extensive library on sexuality and sex related topics.
http://www.sexuality.org/
• STD Information
Information about contracting and treating sexually transmitted diseases.
http://medwww.bu.edu/people/sycamore/std/std.htm

Learning and Memory

- Active Brain Areas in Memory
Interactive site designed to explain how memory works in the brain.
http://www.nimh.nih.gov/events/prfmri2.htm

- Animal Training at Sea World
Site discusses how operant conditioning is used to teach animals to perform at Sea World.
http://www.seaworld.org/animal_training/atcontents.html

- Memory
Interactive site designed to teach classical conditioning, operant conditioning and cognitive learning.
http://www.science.wayne.edu/~wpoff/memory.html

- Observational Learning
Site details Bandura's research on observational learning.
http://www.valdosta.peachnet.edu/~whuitt/psy702/behsys/social.html

- The Psychology of Invention
Site to discover how invention and discovery happen.
http://hawaii.cogsci.uiuc.edu/invent/invention.html

Motivation and Emotion

- Research on Human Emotions
Site defines emotions and how they are measured.
http://www.white.media.mit.edu/vismod/demos/affect/AC_research/emtions.html

- Emotions and Emotional Intelligence
Site about different types of emotions and ways to measure emotional intelligence.
http://trochim.human.cornell.edu/gallery/young/emotion.htm

Neuroscience and Neuropsychology

- Neuropsychology Central
Information of neuropsychological assessment, brain imaging and cognitive psychology.
http://www.premier.net/~cogito/neuropsy.html

- Neuroscience Atlas Images
Images and explanations about the functioning of parts of the brain, spinal cord and the eye.
http://anatomy.uams.edu/HTMLpages/anatomy.html/neuro_atlas.html
- Neurosciences on the Internet
Dedicated to neuroscientific research sites.
http://www.neuroguide.com/

Personality

- Great Ideas in Personality
All major models of personality and relevant research are covered on this site.
http://galton.psych.nwu.edu/GreatIdeas.html
- Personality Testing
Site lists personality tests on-line that the user can take and have scored.
http://www.2h.com/Tests/personality.html

Psychological Testing and Assessment of Intelligence

- Be Careful How You Define Intelligence
Site discusses cross cultural differences in intelligence.
http://www.apa.org/monitor/oct97/define.html
- Down Syndrome WWW Page
Information about risks, diagnosis and symptoms of down syndrome.
http://www.nas.com/downsyn
- FAQ's about Psychological Tests
Site answers most frequently asked questions about psychological testing.
http://www.apa.org/science/test.html
- The Knowns and Unknowns of Intelligence
Provides information about what intelligence is and how it can be measured.
http://www.apa.org/releases/intell.html

Schools of Psychology and Psychologists

- About Humanistic Psychology
  Gives information on the theory, history and future of humanistic psychology.
  http://ahpweb.org/aboutahp/whatis.html
- Alfred Adler
  Learn about Alfred Adler, the founder of Individual Psychology.
  http://ourworld.compuserve.com/homepages/hstein
- Ask Dr. Ellis
  Learn about Dr. Ellis and Rational Emotive Therapy on this Web site.
  http://www.rebt.org/ask.html
- Carl Jung
  Site devoted to information about Carl Jung and his theories of collective consciousness.
  http://www.cgjung.com/cgjung/
- FreudNet
  Library listing the life and complete works of Sigmund Freud.
  http://www.interport.net/nypsan
- Sigmund Freud
  Site discusses Freud's theories and writings on psychoanalysis.
  http://freud.t0.or.at/freud/index~e.htm
- William James
  Dedicated to the works of William James and mind/body psychology.
  http://serendip.brynmawr.edu/Mind/James.html

Sensation and Perception

- How We See
  Easy to understand tutorial about the visual system.
  http://www.gene.com/ae/AE/AEC/CC/vision_background.html
- Interactive Illustrations of Color Perception
  Interactive site to learn about color interactions and color perception.
  http://www.cs.brown.edu/research/graphics/research/illus/spectrum/home.html
- Optical Illusions
  Site provides interesting optical illusions to aid in understanding perception.
  http://www.illusionworks.com/

- Optical Illusions and Paradoxes
  The Escher Gallery provides graphic images of optical illusions and paradoxes.
  http://www/worldofescher.com/

- Perceptual Processes
  Wide-range of tutorials on the process of perception.
  http://onesun.cc.genoseo.edu/~intd225/prcptn.html

- Smell
  Detailed description of the olfaction system.
  http://www.nih.gov.nidcd/smell.htm

- Smell and Taste Disorders
  Site contains frequently asked questions about the olfaction and gustation systems.
  http://www.nih.gov/nidcd/smltaste.htm

Sex and Gender and Psychology of Women

- Androgyny Information
  Information about the incorporation of both masculine and feminine traits.
  http://www.chaparraltree.com/raq/

- Gender and Sexuality
  Provides resources and articles on issues relating to gender and sexuality.
  http://eserver.org/gender/

- Women's Resources
  Dedicated to women's issues and feminine psychology.
  http://www.wwwomen.com/

Social Psychology

- Social Psychology
  Provides articles and links to issues in social psychology.
  http://www.trinity.edu/~mkearl/socpsy.html

- Social Psychology Network
  Site offers resources and links to issues related to social psychology.
  http://www.wesleyan.edu/spn/

• Studying Television Violence
Information about studies conducted on the effects of television violence
on viewers.
http://www.ksu.edu/humec/fshs/tv95.htm

• Violence on Television
Extensive source for information about television and violence.
http://www.apa.org/pubinfo/violence.html

Substance Use and Abuse and Psychopharmacology

• Drugs and Behavior
Provides information about a wide variety of drugs and their effects.
http://www.uwsp.edu/acad/psych/tdrugs.htm

• National Institute on Drug Abuse
Government sponsored page provides information about the legal, health
and treatment issues surrounding drug use.
http://www.nida.nih.gov

• Psychopharmacology Tips
Site to look up psychiatric drugs and their effects.
http://uhs.bsd.uchicago.edu/~bhsiung/tips/tips.html

Additional Resources for Psychology

The following resources are designed to help access a variety of information in the field of psychology. Many of these Web sites were designed
with the psychology student in mind, so they provide links to important
sources, journals, periodicals, and articles related to major issues in this
field.

• Electronic Journals and Periodicals in Psychology
Annotated list of links to psychology related journals, periodicals, and
bibliographies.
http://psych.hanover.edu/Krantz/journal.html

• Human Relations Publications
Site has human relations and human development publications on over
fifty topics.
http://muextension.missouri.edu/xplor/hesguide.humanrel/

- Psych Web
Designed for students and teachers, site is filled with psychology related links.
http://www.psych-web.com/

- Psychology Database
Accesses the search engine maintained by the American Psychological Association.
http://www.psychcrawler.com/

- Psychology Departments Around the World
Comprehensive list of psychology department home pages around the world.
http://psy.ucsd.edu:80/otherpsy.html

- Psychology Links
Links to all types of psychology related sites on the Internet.
http://galaxy.tradewave.com/galaxy/Social-Sciences/Psychology.html

- Psychology Resources
Sites geared toward psychology majors identifying psychology-related information.
http://www.onlinepsych.com/mh/

- The Psychology Study Center
On-line activities and multimedia links to psychology topics.
http://psychstudy.wadsworth.com/index.shtml

Hands-On Assignment

Newsgroups

Newsgroups (see Chapter Two) are a valuable resource both for getting a research idea and for developing that idea to a razor's edge. A listing of Newsgroups specializing in psychology can be found at **http://matia. stanford.edu/cogsci/usenet.html**. The groups include:

- alt.psychology
- alt.psychology.help
- alt.psychology.jung
- alt.psychology.nlp
- alt.psychology.personality
- bit.listserv.ioob-1: Industrial psychology.
- bit.listserv.psycgrad: Psychology graduate student discussions.

- sci.cognitive: Perception, memory, judgement and reasoning.
- sci.psychology: Topics related to psychology.
- sci.psychology.announce
- sci.psychology.consciousness
- sci.psychology.digest: PSYCOLOQUY, a refereed psychology journal and newsletter
- sci.psychology.misc
- sci.psychology.personality
- sci.psychology.psychotherapy
- sci.psychology.reserach: Research issues in psychology
- sci.psychology.theory

Listservs

Listservs are electronically managed mailing lists (see Chapter Two) that may be valuable if you have a specific question or wish to see what questions others are asking. Links to psychology-specific listservs can be found at **http://www.grohol.com/mail.htm**

Hands-On Assignment

As you develop your ideas for a research project, you can search the Web for journal articles, Newsgroups, and other sources of information. Use the search engine that accompanies your Web browser or one of those listed earlier. Remember to make your search as specific as possible to avoid getting an unmanageable number of hits. Another method for searching is to use one of the sites that complies links, such as those listed above. List the search engine or compilation of links used. Then list your chosen topic.

Once you have completed your search, choose the three sites that have information that would be useful to you in developing your research ideas. Write a brief description of each one.

1. URL:

   Sponsor or Author:

   Description:

2. URL:

   Sponsor or Author:

   Description:

3. URL:

Sponsor or Author:

Description:

Doing a Literature Search Online

In addition to the databases outlined in the textbook and available from your university library, the Internet offers a variety of research resources. Many academic libraries allow access to their facilities via the Internet. Doing a search on Yahoo! for the key phrase "academic libraries" will yield an extensive list of libraries, many with their catalogues online: **http://www.yahoo.com/Reference/Libraries/Academic_Libraries**.

The library at Arizona State University **http://www.asu.edu/lib/** is an example of a well-organized and easy-to-use site. Follow the library's "catalogs" link to the online catalog, where you can search the contents of the library by author, title, key word, and more. Remember the principles of efficient searching. Using good search strategies such as more specific key words in combination, you can limit your search to any specific subject. For the key word "psychology" you will find approximately 28,300 titles, but if you limit your search to a combination of "gender" and "preschool" you will find seven titles.

If you want to restrict your literature search to journals, you can access a database of more than 17,000 multidisciplinary journals using a service called Uncover Web at **http://uncweb.carl.org/**. From the opening screen, click on "Search the UnCover Database" and a log-in screen will load.

You may elect to create a profile to personalize search parameters or to create an "Access" account to which you can bill document delivery. You can also search as a guest by clicking the Search UnCover Now button.

For example, entering the term "imitative learning" as a key word produces six results. If the list of articles from your key word search is unwieldy, then you can further define the search by adding terms in the search box at the bottom of the list. You may want to click on any article listed to get details for publication (date and journal number). Write down these details for future reference (that is, so you can find the article at a local library), or order the article for delivery. Remember that there is a charge for the delivery service.

Hands-On Assignment

Using the list of academic libraries, search for your own library or one with which you can arrange an interlibrary loan. Search for your topic and note the publications that are available. List the following items:

- URL of library catalog
- Topic for which you searched
- Number of listings received
- Description of three publications that appear most useful

Working with Research Participants

Using the Internet to Find Participants

An online listing of continuing psychology experiments on the Web can be found at **http://psychological science.org**. In addition to ongoing research currently being conducted, you receive a comprehensive explanation of using the Internet in research design. If you want to learn how to place your own questionnaire online go to "How to Put Questionnaires on the Internet" at **http://salmon.psy.plym.ac.uk/mscprm/forms.htm**.

Hands-On Assignment

Participate in an online psychology experiment. Go to **http://www.psychologicalscience.org** and click on "Psychology Links", scroll to the bottom of the page and find "Other Sites of Interest". In this section you find "Online Psychology Experiments", click on this to see current research being conducted in psychology. Choose one of the experiments that involves answering a survey. After you have participated in the survey, answer the following questions:

1. Was the survey instrument online, or did you have it sent to your e-mail address?

2. How many questions did the survey ask?

3. How long did it take for you to complete the survey?

4. What format was used for the questions?

5. Did you detect any problems or flaws with the questionnaire or the manner in which it was administered?

6. Were you given the option of obtaining a copy of the results of the experiment when the research was completed?

7. What are the advantages or disadvantages to the researcher of using Internet users for participants in an experiment?

8. What might the researcher have done differently in designing his or her experiment?

Analyzing Your Data

Software for Data Analysis

You can obtain software for data analysis via the Internet, as well as general and technical assistance, at the following sites:

• Minitab
  http://www.minitab.com/
• Online Statistical Power Calculator
  http://www.stat.ucla.edu/calculators/powercalc
• SAS Institute
  http://www.sas.com
• SPSS
  http://www.spss.com/
• SPSS and SYTAT List Serves
  http://www.spss.com/tech/listserves.html
• StatView
  http://www.abacus.com/techsupport/techsupp.html

One especially interesting site is **http://www.stat.ucla.edu**. In addition to offering an online statistics textbook, which can be useful for additional explanations of basic concepts such as observation and variables, this site provides a statistics glossary, statistics toolbox, useful formulas, a program that generates random tables, a sample size calculator, and many other handy tools.

Many sites on the Internet provide valuable data for analysis. A search engine using terms such as "psychological datasets" will generate a comprehensive listing.

Hands-On Assignment

It is important for researchers to decide how to analyze their data once it has been collected. Go to the Selecting Statistics section **http://trochim. human.cornell.edu/selstat/ssstart.htm** of the Center for Social Research Methods at Cornell University. Answer the questions there as they relate to the characteristics of a dataset that you need to analyze. Note the results by addressing the following questions:

1. Could you answer all of the questions related to your data?

2. Did you agree with the statistical method suggested for your data?

3. Do you see any advantages or disadvantages to choosing a method of data analysis using a site such as this?

Ethical Issues in Research

In any psychological research project it is important to follow accepted ethical guidelines. The American Psychological Association has established guidelines for psychologists; these are available on the APA Web site at **http://www.apa.org/ethics/code.html**. This detailed code of ethics sets forth principles and enforceable standards for psychologists in a variety of roles and situations. The following sites also cover such ethical issues as finding research participants, sampling, and questioning the validity of research findings:

- Ethics Committee Home Page
  http://www.psych.bangor.ac.uk/deptpsych/Ethics/index.html
  The psychology department of the University of Wales, Bangor, provides
  a sample consent form, bibliography, and additional links.

- On Being a Scientist
  http://www.nap.edu/readingroom/books/obas
  This book from the National Academy of Science discusses responsible
  conduct in research.

Reporting Research Results and Submitting Manuscripts for Publication

The accepted format for reporting results is defined by the American
Psychological Association. The APA maintains an online style guide at
www.apa.org/journals/faq.html. Other sites that offer tips on APA style
include:

- A Guide for Writing Research Papers
  http://webster.commnet.edu/apa/apa_intro.htm
- Guidelines for Writing in APA Style
  http://www.1dl.net/~bill/aparev.htm
- Psychology with Style
  http://www.uwsp.edu/acad/psych/apa4b.htm

Submissions to many journals must meet other requirements besides
APA style guidelines. The Web is also a good source for author instructions, as exemplified by the following sites:

- Author instructions for the *Journal of Experimental Social Psychology*
  http://www.apnet.com/www/journals/js/jsifa.htm
- Author instructions for the *Journal of Personality and Social Psychology*
  http://www.apa.org/journals/pspjnlms.html

INTERNET GLOSSARY

applet   See **Java.**

Archie   A search engine for FTP archives.

ArchiePlex   Web-based interface for using Archie.

ASCII   The basic code e-mail uses; does not allow underlining, italics, etc.

bandwidth   The amount of information that can be transferred across a network at one time.

bit   The smallest unit of information in a computer; represented by 0 or 1; eight bits equal a **byte.**

Bookmark   A tool provided by most Web browsers that enables you to save Web page URLs so that you can return to them at any time.

Boolean logic   A system for searching a database that uses the operators AND, OR, and NOT to look for two variables.

bps (bits per second)   A measure of data transmission capacity, used to describe a modem's speed, such as 28.8 Kbps (or 28,800 bits per second).

browser   An interface for reading information on the World Wide Web, either graphic (such as Netscape or Explorer) or text-only (such as Lynx).

bulletin board (BBS)   Area where users can read and post messages as well as download files.

byte   A unit of information in a computer, equal to 8 bits.

cache   A region of memory where frequently accessed files can be stored for rapid retrieval.

CD-ROM (compact disc, read-only memory)   A compact disk used to store and retrieve computer data.

chat   Electronic conversations among Internet users taking place in real time in chat areas (or chat channels, groups, rooms, or sites).

client   The computer and software you use to access Internet servers.

DNS (domain name system)   The convention for translating the names of hosts into Internet address; see also **URL.**

domain name   The part of the Internet address (URL) that specifies the area on a computer reserved for a particular organization, such as `mayfieldpub.com`. In this example, `.com` stands for "commercial"; other types of organization designations include `.edu` for "educational" and `.gov` for "governmental."

download   To transfer information from one computer to another, or to transfer information from a network to your computer.

e-mail Electronic mail, one of the most popular uses of the Internet, it can be sent to an individual or a list.

FAQ (frequently asked questions) Lists of common questions about a particular product, service, or topic.

file path Subdirectory in a URL, leading to the specific file you want.

flaming Sending a large number of angry messages, usually to someone who has broken the rules of netiquette.

freeware Software you get for free.

FTP (file transfer protocol) The standard protocol for transferring files across the Internet. Most browsers have one-way FTP; for two-way (the ability to send as well as receive), you can acquire FTP software for both Macintoshes (Fetch) and PCs (WS_FTP).

gateway A device whose purpose is to aid in the transfer of packets of information from one network to another.

GIF (graphics interchange format) File format for images that are viewable on the Web; see also **JPEG**.

Gopher A menu-driven information system created at the University of Minnesota.

hits The number of times a particular page is accessed, or the number of successful matches you receive during a key word search.

home page The main, or starting, page for a series of Web pages.

HTML (hypertext markup language) The formatting language of the World Wide Web.

HTTP (hypertext transfer protocol) The protocol for reading HTML programs from the Web.

hyperlink See **link**.

hypermedia Links among various kinds of multimedia objects, such as video, audio, and virtual reality, in addition to text and graphics.

hypertext A text link that takes you to another file on the Internet. A hypertext document contains hypertext, or hyperlinks, or both.

Internet A global network of linked computers; home to the World Wide Web, newsgroups, bulletin boards, Gopher, and online forums.

IRC (Internet relay chat) See **chat**.

ISP (Internet service provider) A company that provides subscribers access to the Internet.

Java Programmed mini-applications ("applets") for Web browsers.

JPEG or JPG (joint photographic expert group) File format for images that are viewable on the Web; see also **GIF**.

Jughead A search engine for Gopher document titles.

link Short for **hyperlink**. A link, text or graphic, that takes you to another file on the Internet or another location in a document.

listserv   A program that distributes e-mail to a mailing list.

lurk   To browse and read messages, but not actively participate in a discussion group. A good idea before joining discussion groups.

mailing list   A discussion group that shares an interest in a particular topic; messages sent by members of the group are e-mailed to all its members.

megabyte (MB)   A unit of computer information storage capacity equal to 1,048,576 bytes.

modem   A device that allows a remote computer to communicate via phone lines to networks and other computers.

MOO (MUD object-oriented environment)   Multiple-user environment based on object-oriented programming technology. See **MUD**.

MUD (multiuser domain [dungeon, dimension])   Virtual environment on the Internet primarily used for role-playing games such as Dungeons and Dragons.

MUSH (multiuser shared hallucination)   A MUD variation.

netiquette   Etiquette on the Internet; the guidelines for preferred behavior when communicating with others on the Internet.

network   A system of computers that can transmit information from one to another.

newbie   Someone new to the Web.

news filter   A software program that lets you customize your news. You can choose what type of news you want and from what source.

newsgroup   A discussion group, or informal bulletin board, that shares an interest in a particular topic; newsgroups are located on Usenet, where articles are read and posted.

packet   When information is transferred from the Internet to your computer, it is broken into packets, or pieces, which are transmitted to your computer and reassembled by TCP software.

page   Any Web document viewable with a browser.

platform   The operating system that your computer runs—for example, DOS (disk operating system), Windows, or Macintosh.

POP (post office protocol)   The standard protocol for reading Internet mail sent using SMTP.

portal   A Web page that combines search engine, subject tree, news filter, etc. Most major search engines now have first pages that are actually portals.

protocol   Information format. The protocol lets two computers know what type of information is being transferred. The protocol for transferring information across the Internet is given in the first part of the URL (e.g., http, ftp, gopher, telnet).

RAM (random access memory)   The amount of available short-term memory in a computer directly correlating to the speed of your processor—the more RAM you have, the faster your computer is.

real-time communication   Communication in which your messages are seen instantly; makes possible "live" conversations.

ROM (read-only memory)   The unchangeable portion of the computer's memory containing the start-up instructions for your system.

route   The path a packet takes from the server to the client.

search engine   A program that allows you to perform key word searches to locate Web documents.

server   A computer accessible to other networked computers.

shareware   Copyrighted software that is distributed on a trial basis; you eventually have to pay for it if you want to continue to use it beyond the trial period. The cost is generally minimal.

SMTP (simple mail transfer protocol)   The standard protocol for transferring e-mail from one computer to another across the Internet.

spam   Unsolicited e-mail usually sent to a large number of users, such as to a Usenet group or a listserv mailing list.

subject tree   A hierarchical directory of information.

surfing   Aimlessly exploring the Internet by clicking links from one page to another.

tags   Codes used in **HTML** (hypertext markup language).

TCP/IP (transmission control protocol/Internet protocol)   TCP is the software your computer uses to create an interface with the Internet. TCP software receives the packets of data transmitted across the Internet and reassembles the corresponding file so that you can view the resulting Web page. IP is the protocol that computers use to talk to each other on the Internet, and it helps to define the route packets take.

Telnet   A standard protocol for logging on to another computer remotely. For example, if you want to log on from home to your UNIX account at school, you can use Telnet.

thread   The original newsgroup message (article) and all of its associated replies.

UNIX   A freeware computer operating system used by many colleges and universities.

URL (uniform resource locator)   An address for an Internet location.

Usenet   A UNIX-based computing system used mainly for discussion and newsgroups.

Veronica   A program that searches the full text of Gopher documents.

videoconference   Two or more people interacting through real-time video and audio feeds.

virus   A self-replicating destructive program that can be downloaded from the Internet or obtained via an infected file on a diskette. A few viruses are harmless and even amusing, but most can destroy the data on your hard disk.

Web page   A document accessible on the Web.

World Wide Web   The segment of the Internet that uses primarily HTTP.

WOO (Web object-oriented environment)   A virtual space primarily used for role playing similar to MUD, but located on the World Wide Web.

INDEX

FAVORITE WEB SITES

Name of Site: _____

URL: _____

Name of Site: _____

URL: _____

Name of Site: _____

URL: _____

Name of Site: _____

URL: _____

Name of Site: _____

URL: _____

Name of Site: _____

URL: _____

Name of Site: _____

URL: _____

Name of Site: _____

URL: _____

Name of Site: _____

URL: _____

Name of Site: _____

URL: _____

Name of Site: _____

URL: _____

Name of Site: _____

URL: _____

Name of Site: _____

URL: _____

Name of Site: _____

URL: _____

Name of Site: _____

URL: _____

Name of Site: _____

URL: _____

Name of Site: _____

URL: _____

Name of Site: _____

URL: _____

Name of Site: _____

URL: _____

Name of Site: _____

URL: _____

Name of Site: _____

URL: _____

Name of Site: _____

URL: _____

Name of Site: _____

URL: _____

Name of Site: _____

URL: _____

Name of Site: _____

URL: _____

Name of Site: _____

URL: _____

Name of Site: _____

URL: _____

Name of Site: _____

URL: _____

Name of Site: _____

URL: _____

Name of Site: _____

URL: _____

Name of Site: _____

URL: _____

Name of Site: _____

URL: _____

Name of Site: _____

URL: _____

Name of Site: _____

URL: _____

Name of Site: _____

URL: _____

Name of Site: _____

URL: _____

Name of Site: _____

URL: _____

Name of Site: _____

URL: _____

Name of Site: _____

URL: _____

Name of Site: _____

URL: _____

Name of Site: _____

URL: _____

Name of Site: _____

URL: _____

Name of Site: _____

URL: _____

Name of Site: _____

URL: _____

Name of Site: _____

URL: _____

Name of Site: _____

URL: _____

Name of Site: _____

URL: _____

Name of Site: _____

URL: _____

Name of Site: _____

URL: _____

Name of Site: _____

URL: _____

Name of Site: _____

URL: _____

Name of Site: _____

URL: _____

Name of Site: _____

URL: _____

Name of Site: _____

URL: _____

Name of Site: _____

URL: _____

Name of Site: _____

URL: _____

Name of Site: _____

URL: _____

Name of Site: _____

URL: _____

Name of Site: _____

URL: _____

Name of Site: _____

URL: _____

Name of Site: _____

URL: _____

Name of Site: _____

URL: _____

Name of Site: _____

URL: _____

Name of Site: _____

URL: _____

Name of Site: _____

URL: _____

Name of Site: _____

URL: _____

Name of Site: _____

URL: _____

Name of Site: _____

URL: _____

Name of Site: _____

URL: _____

Name of Site: _____

URL: _____

Name of Site: _____

URL: _____

Name of Site: _____

URL: _____

Name of Site: _____

URL: _____

Name of Site: _____

URL: _____